Mary Tyler Peabody Mann, Erasmus Schwab

The School Garden

Being a practical Contribution to the Subject of Education

Mary Tyler Peabody Mann, Erasmus Schwab

The School Garden
Being a practical Contribution to the Subject of Education

ISBN/EAN: 9783337073251

Printed in Europe, USA, Canada, Australia, Japan

Cover: Foto ©Andreas Hilbeck / pixelio.de

More available books at **www.hansebooks.com**

THE

SCHOOL GARDEN.

BEING

A PRACTICAL CONTRIBUTION TO THE SUBJECT OF EDUCATION.

BY

PROF. ERASMUS SCHWAB,

DIRECTOR OF THE MILITARY COLLEGE OF VIENNA.

TRANSLATED FROM THE FOURTH GERMAN EDITION BY

MRS. HORACE MANN.

NEW YORK:

M. L. HOLBROOK & CO.

1879.

TRANSLATOR'S PREFACE.

The "School Gardens," by Dr. Schwab, is a little book that seems to come most opportunely to this country, just as the minds of educators are at work upon the problem of industrial education for the young. Industrial education for the adult is quite another matter, and yet its foundations should be laid earlier. Workshops of all sorts are gradually being established, in which various branches of industry may be learned after children leave the grammar school and high school ; but the aim of the school garden is to make the young *love* industrial work—for what we love we do— and there is no introduction to such occupations so charming as the culture of flowers. Thousands of school gardens are in operation in Austria to-day, to say nothing of other places, as the fruit of Dr. Schwab's fertile and comprehensive brain. In preparing this work for the American public, certain adaptations will have to be made to our different institutions of society, and our different plants and birds ; for it is designed for a *manual* as well as for an exhaustive essay upon the subject, in which light it is of world-wide application. Dr. Schwab's own animated words are best for the general consideration of the subject, and the reader will easily see where they do not apply in practice.

MRS. HORACE MANN.

AUTHOR'S PREFACE.

In the autumn of 1866, the citizens of Olmutz begàn to lay out a large park on a plan which I had pointed out to the *Stadtverordereten-Collegium*, as a compensation for the destruction of the public walks by the war. The lively public interest shown in the movement awakened in me, then a member of the Committee for City Improvements, the desire to plant trees and cultivate flowers, and the endeavor to lead others to share in that pleasure. It called out in me many trains of thought, which, according to one of my nature, were destined sooner or later to become acts.

In the year 1870, I was appointed inspector of the German public schools in the Circle of Olmutz.. The excellent new school-law of 1869 decreed that with every country school should be connected an experimental garden, which in another part of the law was called an experimental field (Versuchsfeld). This word was such an unlucky one, so general and yet so narrow, and therefore vague, that a full year passed after the appearance of the law before it was understood or carried into operation. Although an idealist through and through, I was used to results in life, and it delighted me to set at work my little modicum of organizing talent. Two points were clear to me : first, that no peasant would allow his son to undertake such a foolish experiment in the public school as to learn to cultivate a field with plough and mattock ! In the second place, I recognized more and more every day what I instinctively felt on first reading the law : *that there should be, not only for every country school but for every city school,* a pleasure-ground ; per haps still more for the latter than for the former.

WHY I WAS INTERESTED.

I was inspecting one day the school of the little village of Redweis, near Olmutz. The region around it is a fruitful plain, a portion of the well-known Hanna ; but far and wide I saw that, with the exception of the fruit trees of the house garden, there was neither tree nor shrub ; only a few trees in the streets, in a few places. I pitied the children of a village, to whom the contemplation of nature is so circumscribed by the poverty of animal and plant life. As I looked out of the school-room window, I saw, outside of the teacher's garden, only a wide, waste piece. The thought immediately took root in me, "here belongs a school garden!" And with this word I had found the key to what I was seeking. On my way home the idea of what this school garden must be was clear. I went immediately to the manufacturer, Herr Max Machanek, who possesses a happy talent for landscape gardening, which he had made known by his good plan for the city park in Olmutz, and with whom I had been visiting gardens since the year 1866. For, I thought the plan must not only be a good one, it must be beautiful. I developed to the gifted man my thoughts about the different kinds of school gardens which had flashed through my head like lightning. And now we went to work. In eight days this pamphlet of mine was written, which I called "The Public School Garden;" for at that time I did not dare to express aloud that I was thinking of gardens for all kinds of schools. In eight days, Herr Machanek had also three plans ready, one for Redweis, and two ideal ones for villages, and also for small cities.

The pamphlet made a kind of epoch in Austria. People were charmed with the text, and transported with the colored pictures which, at the expense of Herr Machanek, brought out so beautifully, clearly and lovingly, the idea of the school garden suited to time and place. The public reproached both gardeners for having dared to surround nurseries and beds for field produce with neat borders, *i. e.*, with curved lines! As to the rest, they were pleased that the plans, putting to shame the time-honored stiff symmetry of straight lines, and avoiding the taste of modern gardening, had an easy grace and an agreeable harmony. Thus the little pamphlet, plainly the birth of a moment, awakened in geometrical progression the interest of the public for the founding of school gardens.

Tolerably useful school gardens there certainly were here and there in Germany as well as in Austria, before the appearance of the first edition of this pamphlet; but they found no imitators, so that they brought no results except to the person of the teacher. No wonder that many of them soon relapsed into a wilderness and attracted no attention!

But whence this sad experience? On the one side it may be explained by the indifference of the general public, and the apparent want of means for a proper laying out of the gardens, and to the opposition of many communities to any new enterprise, but chiefly to the miserable lack of instruction in the training schools of teachers, which again points back still farther to the miserable lack of earlier school legislation.

On another side, it cannot be overlooked that even in the latest times there was no clear conception of the school garden on German ground in anybody's head, so that no one could come forward with any striking propositions which would interest experts or persuade communities to offer the place and the means to lay out such gardens in reference to local needs, or demand from the teachers the capacity to deduce them from the actual means of instruction and education, without disturbing the corporate organism of the public schools (volksschulen).

Whoever wishes to make plans for founding suitable school gardens must certainly be an idealist and have a heart for the people ; but he must also possess the necessary technical knowledge required ; he must know life, and be acquainted with the public demands by his own inward observations and insight ; he must have had intercourse with all classes of the population, and must especially be acquainted with teachers, and be himself a school man, in order to be able to meet the question whether his plans can reckon upon general sympathy and furtherance.   When the author endeavors five years after the first appearance of his pamphlet to give himself an account of his success, whereby he, setting aside his individual views, has won the general confidence in the correctness and practicability .of his plans, he finds that a concatenation of circumstances has enabled him to solve such a problem.   His studies had the ideal and

also the real life for their subject—an active profession
has made him specially acquainted with many peoples
and countries, and had tempted him, in some sort, to
speak with authority.

In Germany and other places, the author, on account
of this work, has often been greeted as a hopeful pupil
of Froebel, and passes for one still by most people. I
have often related that I came naturally, as it were, by
my idea of the school garden, and have freely confessed
that five years ago I knew little of Froebel. Since that
time I have certainly been much interested in him who,
before my time, had wished for a school garden ; but
before me no one had had the good fortune to make a
propaganda for his plans with any result ; then—were
there any school gardens outside of German ground ?

The " Public School Gardens " of the author undertakes to give the outlines according to which country
and city school gardens should be laid out. According
to the judgment of school-men, naturalists and men of
practical life, not an idea in this pamphlet should be
neglected which can be brought to life by the school
garden.

WHAT IS NECESSARY, AND WHO FAVOR IT.

It is very striking that the school garden, as it is called
to-day, repeatedly emphasizes the fact that not all the
plans are everywhere practicable ; that the necessary
and suitable ones are chosen with tact and understanding ; but as to the rest, especially where there is no
money to be had for the purpose, it must be given up.

According to the advice of the inspector of the court
garden, Jäger, in Eisenach, from whom I have learned
much, it is best that the garden land (grabe land) be

separated from the other garden. Nursery, experimental garden and vegetable garden may be laid out in rectilinear beds, but masked with shrubbery; the other garden should, at least in cities, take more of a landscape character.

The expense, if the ground is a level one, may be only fifty florins; it may be five hundred, indeed, a thousand or more if one is not afraid of the cost. The best argument for meeting the expense is the numerous school gardens, which, according to the ideas laid down in this pamphlet, were newly planned or wholly transformed. The idea of the school garden is a great one in its bearing upon instruction and education; but it is also a fitting and unanswerable one. That national economists and scientifically cultivated land-owners promise the school garden a great future; that naturalists, that medical writers welcome this idea gladly, was apparent from the beginning. Also prominent pedagogues sympathized with the proposals of the author immediately and unconditionally. Letters from the most various portions of Austria and Germany, and from Italy and England, express cordial interest. The periodical and daily press have been equally favorable.

This unanimous support of sober and of enthusiastic, and also of experienced men in all conditions of life, was also shared by the unprejudiced circles in Austria. The Ministry of Instruction in Hungary, all the school inspectors and normal institutions, have taken part in the public school garden, and given it their earnest furtherance. The Royal Imperial Ministry of Agriculture have sent my pamphlet to all their agricultural societies and teachers' institutes, with an invitation to notice it in their official documents. Thereupon the K.

K. (or Royal Imperial) Ministry of Instruction received "The School Garden" for the teachers' library of the public schools, and required of the normal schools the adoption of the practical hints given in the pamphlet. In 1875, the Ministry of Agriculture required the administrators of public property, public foresters, and the specially rich Greek Oriental Religious Fund in Bukowina, to further the founding of school gardens, which requisition already bears fruit. The K. K. Ministry of Instruction has repeatedly granted money to the State Institutions in favor of school gardens. The Ministry of the Interior has also made the K. K. governments cognizant of the bearing upon the welfare of the people and the country of the systematic founding of school gardens as explained by the author.

The agitation for the popular idea of the school garden in Austria has a wide field before it, but the prospect is very favorable. The class of noble landed proprietors has been gained over in most places. For example, the business agent of his highness Duke Albrecht has promised his co-operation in the founding of school gardens upon the numerous domains of this imperial prince, as soon as the teachers show a corresponding ability to do it. In Galicia a very energetic district magistrate has excited the activity of the nobility in his district in a very decided manner. The K. K. Society of Husbandmen in Vienna is ready to promote the interests of school gardens in Lower Austria.

When the normal school of Austria and Hungary shall earnestly, with insight and circumspection, promote the action of the highest boards of instruction, the most important and most indispensable step will have been taken to make the school garden, with all the blessings it will bring, the common property of the people everywhere. The Austrian Board of Instruction, in fact, already admits the laying out of suitable school gardens in several normal school institutions, and the Diet of Lower Austria, by planting school gardens in the pro-seminaries it has erected with so many sacrifices in Vienna, Neustadt and St. Potten, has given a striking example of its comprehension of the idea. But real life already hastens the general founding of school gardens in the normal school institutions. In K. K. Silésia, the Moravian-Silesian Congress of Silk Culture agitated the subject in a striking manner by means of a hand-bill, giving one of my original plans for small country school gardens, and the K. K. Country School Council showed itself as active as it was intelligent. In other countries the practical result of my pamphlet soon manifested itself in the creation of single school gardens.

The Vienna Exposition of 1873 made an epoch for school gardens. The Austrian model school, in whose origin and prosecution the author took an active part, was visited by thousands from all countries, and since this object had the good fortune to excite quite unusual practical results, the subject did not fail of its influence. It pleased numerous friends of schools, and its general diffusion can no longer be a question of any thing but time.

The Country School Counsellor of the Moravians then interested himself in the general diffusion of the school gardens. He demanded the help of the K. K. District School Counsellor, and expressly the State School Counsellor, for their co-operation ; he sought out the Agricultural Society and its sections, and affiliated meetings, for their active support of the measure ; and, in short, he allowed the plans I had published in the two first editions of my pamphlet to be quadrupled and spread about. Other country school counsellors showed themselves friendly to the idea, although in a less energetic manner.

GARDENS ESTABLISHED.

Of the school gardens laid out in the spring of 1874, three deserve special mention. That of the Thomas School, in the Neugasse at Brunn is one, because it proves that room for a school garden can be found in a large city ; a second, in the same city, is added to the orphan house for boys ; and in Vienna, there is one in connection with the training deaf and dumb institution. Both the last are noteworthy, because their aim is to create means of instruction and education for unfortunate children and those deprived of some of their senses. In 1875 the founding of the school garden in the K. K. German Normal School was a specially important measure.

The Society of Public Culture will have a school garden in the most beautiful Alpine regions of Austria. It brought its influence to bear upon the population by a circular which I prepared for them with great pleasure.

FURTHER ENCOURAGEMENT.

That the little pamphlet appeared in its second edition at the Vienna Exposition, and that a fourth is now called for, and that the author has received invitations from foreign countries to pronounce discourses upon the subject, is a proof that at present everywhere the school garden is recognized as the most important foundation of society, and that a good thought, advocated with perseverance, has not to wait long for general co-operation.

The idea of a school garden is already so obviously an acceptable one, that the title of the pamphlet was changed in the third edition from " Public School Garden " to " School Garden." For, it belongs not merely to every public school, but to every school—for the deaf-mutes, for the feeble-minded, for orphans ; to every polytechnic school (real schule), to every gymnasium and every normal school. A specially neat, well-considered garden belongs also to every kindergarten.

School boards will not perhaps everywhere include a garden in a kindergarten, but so much the more should they do so in the public school. In reference to this, the conduct of the K. K. Silesian Board is noteworthy. The School Counsellor recommended the erection of school gardens in a printed document. At present, Diet, Ministry of Agriculture, and Department of Instruction, have granted supplies to every teacher who takes agricultural instruction. These courses of instruction are inspired by local school inspectors, by district school inspectors, and by the votaries of the Agricultural Union, who are appointed by the local school inspector. These last men belong mostly to the class of stewards of landed estates, foresters, proprietors, in short of practical country owners. In the inspection, school gardens are specially considered. If a teacher has not put his school garden into good order, he receives no subsidy.

So long as teachers who have not received instruction upon this subject in their training schools, work in a theoretic, practical way, so long it is recommended, as in Austria, to make them adepts in the matter in the autumn session of the Union. But an adequate course of agricultural instruction for teachers, and agricultural instruction for school children, cannot be thought of without a school garden. In that course given by the Agricultural Ministry, on which the subsidy is dependent, which is held by the indefatigable Director Janovsky, in the six weeks autumnal session of the Union for Silesian public school teachers in the Agricultural Institute at Oberheimsdorf, the founding of public school gardens is made a very prominent feature. In Barrzdorf, half an hour's distance from Oberheimsdorf, the teachers have an opportunity to see a little model school garden. Besides this, Mr. F. Janovsky has already explained how to work out a plan for every school garden in every community of the land, free of expense. The District School Inspectors are also full of zeal, and as soon as they find anywhere, even a partially suitable place which the community will give for a school garden, they send the sketch of the place to Director Janovsky.

IN SWEDEN AND FRANCE.

If the question is at last started whether school gardens already exist in other countries, it must be answered that they exist in Sweden, which to-day numbers two thousand of them. The author first learned this fact in 1871, and in 1873 had an opportunity, as official reporter of the Exposition on the subject of public schools, to look at the Swedish plans. The Swedish school administration is very sound, and the schools are in a high state of development. She has already gone so far in the establishment of school gardens, that she has printed directions which enumerate the plants to be used in them, and gives the proper explanations. On that account, the system is a little one-sided, as their gardens are only established for the country schools, and serve only to spread agricultural instruction. I shall, therefore, show in the proper place, that a great Swedish school garden contains less means of culture than a small one on the Schwab system, as it is called in Austria. It must, however, be granted that Sweden is already beginning to share in such fruits as I wish to show are the after results of the school gardens upon life everywhere. Sweden had a painful experience in the beginning of the enterprise, as the teachers of that time were not taught in their seminaries how to carry them on. Nothing now stands in the way of their universal spread in Sweden.

At the Vienna Exposition in 1873, the author saw the magnificent garden-plans which have beautified so many normal institutes in France. He was assured by a very cultivated French school inspector that France already has many school gardens. I acknowledge that I was not previously in a position to know any thing special about school gardens in France ; for my residence in Paris was before I issued this pamphlet. The French, with their taste and their peculiar talents for gardening of all kinds, have also the gift of contributing a rich share to the formation of the idea of the school gardens.

The school garden needs to-day in every country only some advocates of intellect and organizing talent to be before the end of the century participated in by the commonwealth of European nations. In my view it is nothing but a not yet recognized, yet precious inheritance of the eighteenth century.

In Austria the idea of the school garden has already become so popular that in building new school-houses the rule now is to appropriate one room for the future school garden.

THE SCHOOL GARDEN.

CHAPTER I.

" Nature is our home ; to be a stranger in it brings loss and disgrace to us."

A SCHOOL GARDEN TO EVERY SCHOOL.

The degree of carefulness which a community applies to the education of youth, and consequently to its public schools, is the surest measure of the moral and spiritual standpoint and the political ripeness of the people. The teacher's ability and independence, as well as his favorable, material and social position, is a security for public prosperity, culture and freedom. The public school, as the planting ground of the welfare of the nation, must therefore be the darling of the community. That it is already so where the task of the school has been recognized by the people, is expressed by the school building itself. In every village where it is the pride of the villagers, it is the most beautiful and convenient house in it.

The school house, like the church, must be a " sacred " place ; but it can only be so when it has a suitable location and surroundings. It should have an agreeable, well-cared for approach, a worthy exterior

2

and a convenient interior united ; and when space and neatness, and an abundance of light and air are added, it will be made the dearest resort of youth.

Great and difficult in our day is the task of the public school. The requisition is to educate well-instructed, thinking men ; minds prepared for the exigencies of life ; self-governing men, possessing sentiments of duty and honor, love of their fellow-men, and the power of self sacrifice—in short, characters useful to the community.

How can the school reach this ideal?

In the cities of Austria there is at present no child that does not enjoy high instruction, for eight long years, in from five to eight different classes. The teacher, since he has before him only children of the same age, can in this long period of time, if his classes are not overburdened with numbers, attend to the individual needs of each child ; and the child learns from such studies as natural philosophy and geography, so much for the uses of life that he must be incomparably far in advance of the child of the country regions. He then enters a *bürger schule.* This has been the case with the majority of the children in tolerably large cities. So many cultivating and educating elements are offered them in the school, apart from positive branches of knowledge, that the scholars far outstrip the country child in preparation for life by a greater intellectual maturity, capacity for acquisition, and self-reliance. In the city, a good teacher of the upper classes will take time to draw the attention of his pupils to the manifold occupations of men, accompanying them to the workshops of the tradesmen and the halls of the manufacturers. In his *Wahrheit und Dichtung,* one may read what Goethe learnt in his youth in this manner, and how much importance he assigned to this instruction by observation.

PURPOSE OF THE SCHOOL.

What compensation can the country school offer to the village child for the lack of the manifold incentives which the fortunate child of the city finds in family and school, and in the many-sided influences of city circumstances ? The goal of education is certainly the same for the city and the country school in all essentials. But how different in reality is the shaping of the knowledge and capacity acquired by the one or the other, as to choice, measure and treatment. This difference is unavoidable, but it surely is necessary only in a certain degree. If it is apparent even in the double class school (schools with two teachers), how much more pronounced must it be in the school of one class, which is the rule in the country, in so many large districts. Here the instruction of the whole offspring of the community, and not of one generation alone, rests upon the shoulders of one man. Ponder this thought, and one will be obliged to confess that this problem is one of the weightiest, most unanswerable and difficult to solve of our day.* Since the education of the people even in cities can only be effected in the midst of an abundance of power and means of instruction and exciting influences, by the concentration of great, well-organized efforts extending over years, the question arises : Is not every patriot, every friend of youth and man in duty bound to think what are the means by which the public school, whether in city or country, shall reach its goal

---

* This difference does not exist in America.—TR.

of broadening the culture of the people in a manner worthy of human destiny?

There is a key to the solution of this problem, and it is found essentially in a just estimate of the value of instruction in *natural science.* Rossmüssler expresses himself thus: " Mother Earth, with her materials, powers, phenomena and forms of life is to us what we call *nature.* This nature is our home, to be a stranger to which brings disgrace and injury to us all. In this conception, nature is the ground-work of human culture and morals. In these words, in my view, lies the central point of human instruction."

The shortest, nearest path to this goal is the establishment of school gardens suited to time and place. In the school garden may be comprised far more than half of the instruction in natural history and science, and specially an essential part of the science of the home region. Here and there good school gardens are found in which this or that department of natural history has been taught with more or less skill, and which have served to diffuse many useful and good thoughts. But school gardens which seek to flow in all directions into a unified, well thought out, consecutively progressive whole, with a plan and purpose (all that is good and much that is excellent that is found scattered here and there without reference to a greater sphere), were set in motion by the two first editions of the " *Volksschulgarten,*" and by the Austrian model school in the Exposition of 1873.

School gardens must certainly always take into view first the manifold circumstances; but they can only solve the pending problems to the thinkers when they follow out not merely single points of view, but. starting from a verified, clear, sound and great thought, set their aim only so high as appears to be attainable in a human way.

The reason why hitherto few endeavors have been made to impart to the people, and especially to the inhabitants of country regions, the magnificent acquisitions of natural science, are, first, that the importance of such knowledge to the people has not been sufficiently recognized ; secondly, that the teaching material for this instruction has not been properly prepared ; thirdly, that the means for personal observation have been wanting.

OUR DEPENDENCE ON NATURE.

But the recognition is making its way that the knowledge of the powers of nature, of its manifestations and its elements, is in a high degree desirable for the so-called *common man*, since, upon· the right use of the elements of nature depends the welfare of the whole people. Much has been done also to popularize natural history in the last decade. Bock's excellent popular work, "Structure, Life and Care of the Human Body," covers the ground of the school wherever the German language is taught ; and German acuteness and the German faculty of teaching have already produced many valuable means of instruction, but,

> "The forward glance to tasks as yet unwon,
> Obscures from view the little man has done."

Yet the importance of instruction in natural history, so far as it shall benefit the man of the country regions, is viewed, at first, only from the standpoint of its utility, and thus far, very one-sidedly. One-sidedly, in so far as this knowledge is declared to be merely useful, not

as absolutely necessary to him whose existence is bound
to nature by a thousand inseparable bonds. He is, indeed, dependent upon it in all and every thing, over
which he is to be master in many points, and upon
which his activity is to be directed. For while nature
must be his friend, and an open book for counsel, instruction and warning, it to-day is in fact locked up
from him by seven seals.

But the knowledge of the natural sciences is to the
man of the country regions, not only necessary for future practical value, and as a point of union for later
progress in useful knowledge, but it may and must serve
him precisely as the groundwork of a universal human
culture. And here we stand before one of the weightiest problems of the modern school garden, before the
known systematic use of the educating element that lies
in the natural sciences, for which, so far as it concerns
the education of the masses, the magic wand is to be
found in no other way.

THE GARDEN SCHOOL A PLACE TO BE HAPPY.

That this use of natural history for educational purposes may and must be begun in school gardens, it is
the design of the following pages to show. A proper
school garden may, must, and is destined to be the
place where children are happiest ; it must be the dearest spot in those hours which they do not spend in the
school room or occupy at home in work for the school.
To be shut out from the instruction and plays of the
school garden will necessarily be one of the most painful punishments to the child. The school room (and
also the little school workshop) and the school garden
are to be the whole world of the child when this is not

furnished by family life ; I mean the world of feeling and intellect, the world of his thoughts, of his childish strivings, of his dreams of future activity. The eye and heart of the child shall open here to the beauty of nature, from the lowest steps of learning, and at the tenderest age ; the attention will be first powerfully excited and fastened here ; the sense of order, purity and neatness, the sense of poetical harmony, and the intuition of beauty must here fall, fertilizing, upon the young soft soul. Here the interest in the manifestations, charms, and treasures of home nature may be awakened, increased and refined ; and here the cherishing and spiritual power of insight can be reached. The pleasure of observing carefully and quietly must be sharpened, in order that the child may reflect upon what is seen, that he may find the connection between effect and cause ; and here the faculty of sifting and rearranging the manifold forms and changing appearances of nature, will be cultivated. But clearness of representation is the first condition for the intellectual work of human life. The school garden will be peculiarly a school of correct and specific judgment, of circumspect reflection, a fountain of the purest and most innocent joys of children and youth,—a communion with nature.

ESTHETIC RESULTS.

Can these educating results cease during life? Must not all the children so trained remain friends of the trees and the flowers they loved ; and, therefore, will they not be the friends of nature, and on the way to be good men ? Will not the destroyer of trees and the tormentor of animals cease in the earth? Will not the life-long effects of the pleasures enjoyed in the beauty of creation, and in the improvement gained in the school garden, express themselves in the character? Surely a new race will thus issue from the schools, a race which will not look upon the earth as a vale of tears, but as a place worthy of human industry, a beloved, habitable home, in which the man of clear mind and joyous heart shall strive and work for his own and his neighbor's happiness.

Will not intellectual minds and moral qualities be developed delightfully by rational school gardens ? - The groundwork of all civil (and human) virtues is the *community*. Heretofore the man from the country has enjoyed less of the feeling of community than the inhabitant of the city, which is not wonderful, since the city is the home of intellectual and moral culture. But where could the germs of *community* be planted more securely and vigorously than in the school garden? There is found not only the common learning of the school, but common work, common pleasure, and common play. By exciting the sense of the community the school garden helps essentially to solve the problem of the people's education. The feeling of inter-dependence will lead to common action with the neighbor, to companionships and friendships for life, laying the foundations of truly brotherly relations among the frequenters of the school. When once the men in a community shall have more pleasing and worthy recollections of their common youth than the dancing floor and the parade ground—not rarely the only recollections they now have in common —when they shall think of the sisterly relations, so to speak, in the school, even of its exciting emulations,— then a public spirit will be kindled and take root. The clear perception that the community is a great family with an inseparable bond of union, does not proceed so much from the school room as it will from the school garden, where intercourse is unrestrained, and which can be seized and felt by the soul of the child in all its depths. These school gardens should belong also to orphan asylums and to those schools which children frequent who are not yet of an age to attend the manufacturers' schools ; they will be under the care of the wife of the teacher, who can also take charge of the instruction of the little girls in womanly occupations, when once the school garden has the necessary enlargement for this purpose. A good school garden will also offer for the instruction, by observation, of little children, the richest and best material, and give them an opportunity to become acquainted with the plant world for common and practical purposes. It will destroy superstition in the people, battle with quackery, help to banish improvidence, cultivate love of nature and confidence in her teachings.

A PROBLEM OF EDUCATION SOLVED.

A judicious and well planned school garden will surely solve an essential part of the problem of the people's education, and help to educate an intelligent and circumspect working power, which, accustomed to ask the *what* the *how* and the *why* upon every subject, will cultivate a correct judgment upon those things and relations in life with which they have to do. It will cultivate also reflective and active natures, from whom sullenness and indolence stand aloof, who have made their own a powerful and persevering will, because they have learned thoroughly by their little labors in the school garden to do in an orderly and capable manner whatever they have to do.

The school garden will not only take care of the general education of the children ; but will do duty on other points, for scientific instruction forms only a part of the instruction of the people. A lively moral feeling and a sound religious direction are impressed by it upon the youth, and thus the public school may turn out a race so virtuous, brave and thrifty through independence, as it would be difficult to produce without the help of so beneficent an aid to progress as a good school garden.

CHAPTER II.

THE SCHOOL GARDEN A PART OF THE SCIENCE OF HOME AND NATURE.

No one who knows the world and men will fail to see that these incitements which are destined to determine the activity of men for their whole lifetime, are the most effectual for individuals as well as for the whole race, if they are brought to bear upon the naïve, freshly receptive age of from six to fourteen years. The understanding seizes them in play, the fancy receives them gladly as material and nourishment for future activity ; enjoyment soon lays the foundation for persistent pursuit and love of them, and for future salutary use of them. The lasting influence of such youthful impressions received under judicious guidance and in the right way, is incalculable.

No intelligent man would make an agricultural school out of the village school, and thereby deprive the public school of its peculiar character ; but is it rare for men to feel that they have not estimated highly enough the incentives received in early youth for industrial and technical activity ? In love of art and science, and all the means of acquiring a reasonable degree of the power to cultivate the earth, and the activities and callings connected with it they feel a deficiency where the country child is early led to. *think* and to prepare for his future life occupation. Let us here ponder upon the saying, *Non scholæ sed vitæ !* Not for the school, but for life !

Ignorance, prejudice and imperfect action have for centuries inflicted wounds upon agriculture. In all lands the power of custom and of inherited privilege falls heavily upon the rural population. Whence shall come help and salvation ? In order to enlighten and cultivate this rural population, the elements of agricultural instruction must, within certain wise limits, be brought into the public school. Well directed schools, but before all things a correctly arranged, progressive course of agricultural instruction, will make the small landholder and the rural workman capable of profiting by good popular agricultural books. This improvement will cost little, and country towns and State will willingly defray the expense.

The country public school *can* bring in this elementary knowledge without neglecting aims of its own, elsewhere recognized in this essay, but it *must* do this if the State comprehends rightly the interests of its tax-payers. Even the smallest village school can solve this problem, and at surprisingly little cost.

WHAT AN EXPERIMENT GARDEN DOES.

The country school already, by law, contains a portion of the school garden, the little " experiment garden for boys." This experiment garden has in general a three-fold aim. It serves in the first place for the cultivation of useful plants of all kinds—cereals, and economic plants, fodder plants, leguminons and hoe-plants, also the different commercial plants ; secondly, for elementary exemplification of the progress in husbandry ; for instance, making beds of a few square meters in circumference, and for the diffusion of the knowledge of physics and chemistry so indispensable to the husbandman. The "experiment" garden serves the younger children for personal observation and ratification of what is communicated to them by instruction, and also for the benefit of outsiders who come to listen to the progressive course of agricultural instruction. It would be very short-sighted to found an insufficient, ordinary agricultural school for the small farmers and day laborers, and leave the mass of the country people unprovided for.

If the public-school teacher does not possess sufficient knowledge to furnish the progressive course of agricultural instruction, the school garden can take in an itinerant agricultural teacher as a guest, and the town shall thus save the money which a special garden for this purpose would cost.* To this "experiment garden" for boys also belongs, in the agricultural department of the school garden, a kitchen garden, an experiment garden for girls, and a nursery for trees.

If there is sufficient space near the school, let the school garden be joined to the school. This is very desirable. If the space is too small for that, the parish can give some waste spot in its territory,—and there are enough such places in the mountainous regions,—which should be near the school if possible. Or it may bestow a little piece of land for this purpose in the neighborhood of the village. This piece of ground must of

---

* It is the custom for "wanderers," or itinerant students, to travel about for a year after they have completed studies in Germany, in order to gain experience.

course he hedged in safely in order to be guarded against injury. The seeds required can be purchased by several united parishes, and if necessary by a whole district (Bezirke), so that each parish will have to contribute but a few kreutzers. In many, probably in most cases, the seeds and plants will be given by public-spirited men and societies, or by other school gardens. Thus, in a surprisingly short time many new, useful plants will be contributed and acclimated, whose domestication would otherwise be difficult and perhaps impossible, unless some large landed proprietor in the neighborhood makes a beginning. New kinds of cereals, maize, saffron, potatoes, hops, the different kinds of table pumpkins so little estimated at their true value, clover (in Hungary), and a series of technical and economical and commercial plants can thus be introduced into many places with little trouble and little cost. Although the more important commercial plants, (that is, medicinal plants,) and those that yield oil, colors, spinning material and roots, give a specially good revenue, the difficulty of their introduction has stood in the way of their general spread, while the consequently little revenue they have brought under these circumstances has led to the abandonment of the endeavor after a few trials.

THE MICROSCOPE AS AN AID.

The microscope, which naturally comes into the service of the public school, will do its part to teach the pupils how to know many dangerous diseases that assail cultivated plants, such as wheat, potatoes, etc., and will make known many scarcely visible insects that are the enemies of agriculture and must be fought.

The improvement of former methods of husbandry will go hand in hand in the rising generation, with the introduction of new cultivated plants and their proper handling in the school garden ; much injurious routine work inherited from the forefathers will fall into disuse ; many wholesome innovations will make their way, and formerly despised or carelessly rejected material will be duly estimated. In many countries esteemed for their husbandry, the cow manure which is allowed to run to waste and to poison the air in so many of our villages, is made good use of. All kinds of manure must be preserved in the school garden in as small a space as possible, to be used by young and old for single plants. Its value is held, alas, very low in almost all parts of Austrian Hungary.

IMPROVEMENT OF THE SOIL.

The ground soon will be made much better and more profitable if this matter of its dressing is attended to, than it now is in most places ; in the neighborhood of cities especially, the village will assume more and more the character of richly remunerative garden culture. Where garden culture already prevails, it will be extended and improved, and in some places where at present it is supposed to be impossible, it will cover the present nakedness, as for instance in many a woodland or mountain village. Where early frosts make impossible the early transplanting of garden growths, the children of the school garden can be taught not to lay out their beloved hot-beds, but to use the much cheaper leaf-mould beds which do their duty much more surely, because, being set later in the year, they give out young plants suitable for the mountain regions at the

proper time.*   Children can be taught in winter to raise
seeds in egg-shells and thumb pots to be planted out
in spring at the right time.

School gardens are the only places where improvements in the culture of the grape-vine by manuring,
pruning and other treatment can be well introduced.

FRUIT CULTURE.

Very special care should be bestowed upon fruit culture in the school gardens. This is as yet too little esteemed as a source of agricultural prosperity. The
school garden can further this interest by cultivating
valuable fruits, raising them from seed and thus accli-
mating foreign fruit, and making every region a fruit
growing one. The school garden should provide a nursery for trees cultivated from wild stock, and quinces,
which improve greatly by good care ; it should also contain trellis fruit of all kinds. Where fruit culture is yet
scarcely known, the husbandman should learn that a
tree that can be bought for 10 neugroschen will soon

---

* Small boxes made of hard burned clay for covering plants are made without
bottoms, and have a straight sloping roof, and an arrangement to hold the glass
safely in its place. Their chief use is to protect the plants from the winter's cold.
By the help of these, cauliflower, cabbage, savoy, salad and other kitchen plants,
can be wintered, if, in the autumn, the boxes are placed in rows two feet apart in
a protected place, and either seeded or planted, the spaces between the boxes
filled with leaves or straw-manure, and protected on the glass side with covering,
in severe frost. In the spring they can be used to protect tender plants that are
then set out, against night frost, rough wind and beating rain, or to lay over vegetables and flowering plants in the open field, and especially in gardens where
there are no hot beds. Most vegetables do better in them than in hot-beds, because in the latter plants are apt to be too much forced. They are particularly
useful for cucumbers and melons when first growing. They may also be used in
summer and autumn to bring forward the settings of woody plants, or to shade
seeds from the heat of the sun, from drought, from snakes, birds or cats, which
last trample down the beds. In winter they are useful for plants that it is hard
to make grow, and that yet do not bear much moisture. They are easily handled.
The glass can be partially removed to let in air, a little from the ground.

represent a capital of from 55 to 130 thalers, for a table-fruit tree easily gains yearly from 4 to 5 florins, and a nut-tree 10 florins. He should be made aware that many endeavors to raise fruit have failed hitherto only because the right kinds were not chosen, or small trees have been brought from good soil to worse, from warm regions to colder ones, from protected situations to exposed ones, etc. In short, failure has come because essential mistakes were made in the beginning, or rational treatment was wanting, or other great errors were committed. When the great advantage which is to be reaped from fruit culture is once seen, and there is sound instruction given about the selection and proper care of trees fitted to the soil and circumstances, fruit trees will be planted everywhere.* When this is the case, the home garden will be taken better care of, dwarf fruit trees will be found harmless to other garden plants, and birds, the exterminators of injurious insects, will come to our gardens.† Soon mountain slopes and waste places will be cultivated with fruit trees, farm fields will be surrounded with them, and streets, lanes, ridges, dams, the shores of brooks and the edges of ponds will be ornamented with them. Respect for the property of others will soon arise when all land proprietors cultivate fruit on their own premises.

TREE PLANTING.

Nor must school gardens forget to plant forest trees. Wherever the woods do not stand very near the school,

---

* It is well to remember that while apple trees are devoured almost bodily by canker worms in Cambridge, the soil is specially adapted to pear trees, which the canker worms do not attack.—TR.

† Cats must be abolished in city gardens to ensure the visitation of birds.

there should be at least one representative of our twenty-five or thirty kinds of trees in the school garden, and also a collection of our most important wild shrubs, if the wood does not actually look into the school windows. If it is not possible to plant trees near the school, one of the village streets can be planted with a row or an alley of trees ; but care should be taken that no two trees of the same kind stand together, as the effect will not be picturesque. Many new trees will be introduced by means of the school gardens—for example, the invaluable larch, the quickly growing ailanthus (God's tree), acacias and Scotch firs on the Hungarian steppes, etc. If the landed proprietors will learn something of the care of forest trees, they will no longer strip the woods of their fallen leaves for litter for their cattle, nor tear away the roots from every fallen tree, for they will know that they are withdrawing the nourishment of the woodlands, which consists of the remains of the rotten and mouldered vegetation. The public school must implant in the children the love of trees, make clear to them what part the woods fulfil in the household of nature, and of what importance they are to man. It must awaken in them the conviction that bad wood-husbandry is the ruin of agriculture, and that short-sightedness for one or two harvests often turns a woodland into an unfruitful waste.

One of the most important of the shrubs which are to be domesticated by the school garden is the willow ; particularly the fine willow that is used for basket making, which will furnish material for the school work-shop and create a lucrative branch of industry for adults. The culture of the willow is very simple, very profitable, and makes it possible to bring empty places, which otherwise would be useless, to a good revenue, since a two or three year old willow-stock will earn from 270 to 310 florins an acre under favorable circumstances. The valuable kinds of willow are well known to be suitable for industrial and agricultural purposes.*

---

* The chief forester, Geyer, in Karlshafen, on the Weser, uses the white willow and its varieties, the silver and gold willow, for margins of shores, hedges of meadows and shade for cattle pastures. The hurdle and basket manufactories use the purple and basket, or garden willow, with their varieties, the almond and spurge-laurel willows. Mountain scarps, moist and low-lying fields, and islands that are periodically submerged, are used for these growths. One morning in Hanover, Geyer counted 30,720 saplings, and reckoned an annual gross income of from $60 to $80 from a capital of about $19. Such plantations last from 18 to 20 years. The rubbish from the peeling (rind and leaves) furnish when dried a good winter fodder for sheep and goats. The *salix caspica* affords very good osier twigs for binding, and grows in dry, clayey, sandy ground from six to eight feet high. This and *salix viminalis* are the best worth cultivating. In the forest and on the shores of rivers, they now use in Prussia in great masses the öder-willow, particularly for binding together pine slabs two feet in width, which are placed one and one-half feet apart for pheasants' closes, for which they are preferred before all other kinds. Willows of three years old are also used by coopers for hoop-staves, and those of two years old by basket makers. The soil for willows must be dug certainly one and one-half feet deep, and must be sandy ground, even gravelly, with clayey subsoil. In pure clay or loam or with moist subsoil they do not make those strong twigs. Ground free from weeds is necessary for willows. On the shore here (of the Danube) were gathered in the tree nursery well-rooted plants set a year ago ; but, in the forest, on the contrary, two year old wood was taken, which is the best for that place, since it is so easily rooted, and one year old wood does not give such strong plants and handsome twigs.

CHAPTER II.

The school gardens will contain at least a few mulberry trees wherever the raising of silk worms is possible or called for.   But it cannot be denied that the cultivation of fruit is the most desirable, and that this had better be well established before the silk culture is attempted.

The school garden, while attending to what is necessary and useful, must be sure not to neglect what is beautiful and pleasant for the children, and must not fail to provide beautiful flowers by which the sense of color shall be awakened in them.   The culture of flowers must be looked upon as instructive, educational and moral in its effect.   Where the school garden is necessarily too small for other things, only flowers must be raised.   The point to be aimed at is that the children shall love their work.

The incentive to gardening will be. still more powerful, if ornamental shrubs are included, which may be planted singly or united in a pretty shrubbery.   Where there is water in a school garden, or very near it, inter-

(36)

esting water-plants must not be forgotten. The influence of the school garden will increase just in proportion as the knowledge of our home plants, and those that can be made home plants by being acclimated, is extended.

And not merely the knowledge of the home *flora*, as far as it can be brought within the sphere of the school garden, but of a portion of our *fauna*—that is of the lower forms of animal life—should be kept in view. The garden and its surroundings give abundant opportunity for the knowledge and observation of the insect world and its interesting transformations. If it is possible to have a little basin in the garden, or if water is near at hand, there is open to the teacher a rich source of information upon the remarkable lower insect world of the water. And as the flowers among plants, so stand the birds among animals, nearest to the heart of children. In large school gardens the thorn hedges afford protection to the singing birds, and hedges in the neighborhood must serve the purpose for the small school gardens.

PRACTICAL OBJECT LESSONS.

Not the school room but the school garden will spread correct views upon the subject of our animals. The future husbandman and gardener, and the future forester, will desire to know the friends and enemies which those denizens of meadow, field and wood as represented in the school garden, possess in the animal world. The hedgehog, for example, will be allowed to dwell undisturbed in the garden; the toad, at present purchased by the English gardeners, will be allowed in the school garden, if it can be kept from the beehives ; for it is otherwise harmless as well as useful. The bats will be spared ; even the buzzards and the owls will be secure as soon as the village youth know that we have only two birds of prey, the hawk and the magpie. The birds will then find protection; gentle hands will strew food for our singing birds during the winter, and the laws which aim to protect these friends of man will be respected. The destroyer of nests and the bird catcher will cease from among men. The singing of birds will enliven the earth and awaken agreeable and friendly feeling where it is now wanting. The titmouse, if unmolested, will increase incredibly, and many useful birds—starlings and jackdaws for instance—will be invited to domesticate themselves by little breeding-houses where they have been seen hitherto only as fleeting guests. Breeding houses for birds belong to school gardens as truly as salt does to bread, or a cup to the social meal.* The few examples mentioned which do not claim to be exhaustive in number, may suffice to show that the school garden can draw within the sphere of its direct and indirect activity a considerable part of the animal world of the home region.

---

* It has been calculated that the blue titmouse daily consumes at least three-quarters of an ounce of butterfly's eggs, and that this amounts to between 15,000 and 20,000 caterpillars. This little bird, then, destroys in one year six and a half millions of such injurious insects! Every pair of titmice brings up yearly from twenty-four to thirty-two young, and if the nourishment of these last amounts to only half that of the old birds, it gives the consumption of the monstrous sum of twenty-four millions of injurious insects by a single family of tom-tits. A cuckoo destroys more than a hundred caterpillars in an hour ; a red-start about six hundred flies ; and innumerable such examples can be found. By the killing of one cuckoo, one titmouse, or one finch in the district inhabited by such a bird, as many pecks or other measure of injurious insects as correspond to its wants, will be let loose upon the vegetation.

A TASTE OF ANIMATED NATURE.

But the school garden will often give an opportunity to introduce new animals whose breeding will be an advantage. In many places the raising of silk worms and of the oak-spinner (a spider) can be introduced. (Pastor Liha at Lukow, in Moravia, earned in 1869 not less than 800 florins by raising oak-spinners.)

In many countries, and in many parts of all countries, a rich revenue may easily be gained by the raising of bees. The bee industry has deteriorated in many countries where it formerly flourished—in the Zips of Hungary, for instance—and yet the demand for wax is such that much has to be imported into Austria. Sugar, which has supplanted honey for the table as a sweetener in all countries but Hungary, does not make so pleasant or so healthy an article of nourishment. The prejudice of many countries in regard to the supposed impossibility of introducing bee culture, throws it specially into school gardens. Bee pasturage is by no means impossible by its limited culture on the plains, and it is even practicable in mountain regions, or indeed not so difficult. Lindens, acacias, fruit trees, chestnuts, will in future be cultivated in every village. For the fruitful plains grow maize, and the bee-nourishing clovers. For these, particularly the white clover, are abundant, and bring much revenue. Hazel bushes, nut trees, whortleberries, Norway maple, willows that stand half way in the water, sunflowers, which find so many uses and are such excellent disinfectants of unhealthy regions, offer fine bee pasturage, and one of the most striking but not well known fodder plants for bees (I mean mignonette), blooms the whole year round. Let a beehive and a bee keeper (Bienenvater) be given to the best scholar, as they do in German Bohemia, and the certain propaganda is sure and rapid.

A GLIMPSE INTO MINERALOGY.

The school garden, which is apparently only for the cultivation of plants, but which really offers muchmaterial for instruction in the animal kingdom, and illustrates the interchanging relations between the vegetable and animal kingdoms, stands also in close relation to many parts of the mineral kingdom, which can have but limited attention in the public school. Since the instruction in all branches must be brought into the most intimate relation with each other, it can also take into view the allied branches of natural science. Here particularly comes in the agricultural science of the soil which treats of its composition, varieties, trial and improvement. The ground principles of physics and chemistry belong to this instruction in natural history, and are quite comprehensible by the younger village children, but will be best understood when they find concrete application. The different branches of natural science taught in the practical garden of the boys may be indicated by various topics. The origin of the humus in the ground by the decomposition of plants and of animal secretions and remains, whence are developed carbonic acid and ammonia; the absorbing of the carbonic acid from the moist soil by the roots of plants, and from the atmosphere by the pores (or lungs) of the leaves; the decomposition of the carbonic acid by the green parts of the plant, under the influence of light, into pure carbon and oxygen; the separation of these

elements ; the mutual influence of the vegetable and animal kingdoms ; the ammoniacal contents of the soil, the
air and the rain water ; the absorption of nitrogen or
azote from the atmosphere ; the absorption of mineral
matter dissolved in the ground and in water ; the origin
of these by mechanical and chemical solution ; the grad-
ual impoverishment of the soil ; the enriching of the
soil by letting it lie fallow, as by manuring it ; the
nature and purpose of manure ; the illustration of the
origin and processes of the nourishing and growth of
plants ; the principles of plant culture ; seed and plant
nurseries, etc. To the observations of the school garden belong elementary experiments in cultivating plants
in water and in sand, together with experiments in the
analysis of the nourishment, germination and multipli-
cation of plants. Probably no one will deny that all
this belongs to the instruction of a well arranged village
school.

Where, for example, can the function of the air in the
economy of nature be better shown than in the open air,
in nature, in the school garden ? Where could the importance of water, the ever present proteus-formed, all
encompassing, all moving, all containing, and all shaping water, the element by whose existence the earth is
what it is, by whose means plants and animals live,
without which we could not exist or improve in cultivation,—where can the importance of light and warmth be
better explained than in the school garden ?

Outside of pedagogic reasons, the chief portion of
the study of natural history falls to the share of the instruction of the public school. Within this field the first
place belongs to the most agreeable part, the plant
world, and not merely because it is the most easy of

comprehension, but for many other reasons, amongst which the most weighty may be that it affords exact, living and repeated material for observation, and because the school child can *live* this knowledge in the most delightful manner in the school garden. Among all the objects of nature, the analogy with the spiritual life of man can be most beautifully shown in plants. But this instruction, given in the spirit of Lüben, is scarcely to be thought of in a public school without the accompaniment of the garden. It is not natural history alone that is exemplified by this mode of instruction ; geography and geology, numbers, language, may all be collaterally taught, a rich nourishment for mind and heart.

The school garden will then, as has been shown, follow up the instruction in natural science in a prominent manner. First for purposes of the special instruction in purely empirical relations with definite practical ends, and aiming also at universal logical considerations, while it holds up to correct thinking ; but it will also serve the purposes of education, while it gives to the child's feelings a truly ethical (or moral) and a healthy æsthetic direction, and cultivates a sense of beauty which, when a grown man, he will be conscious of through his whole life, and manifest in his thinking and acting.

A CITY NECESSITY.

The conviction will be impressed upon the attentive reader that the village school can scarcely take adequate care of the education of the people in the spirit of the nineteenth century without the addition of the school garden. But the city school, where it is possible, must also have its school garden, if it is only a few square meters in circumference ; and, if in the worst case, it can only offer to the children in the most modest manner the opportunity of observing the organism of the development and natural history of plants by means of quite a few well-chosen examples.

Even in the city, the school garden need not be in any sense a peculiar botanical garden or teach any novelties. Its aims should be not instruction in botany, but in the characteristic plants of the home ; to introduce the children not to the science of nature, but to nature itself. And its object should be not merely to bring the plant world near to the children, or to impart directly the knowledge of natural history, but to take advantage of those cultivating and educating moments for the welfare and healing of the rising generation which lie in the province of a knowledge of natural history, and which, alas, are not recognized or improved by all teachers, by which insensibility this instruction is often aimless. The·goal of the city school garden with reference to *education* is the same in its nature as that of the country ; and, even if individual aims of instruction fail, in their places others step forward, not less important in their kind for the city child.

THE CITY AND COUNTRY SCHOOL CONTRASTED.

City and country school gardens cannot possibly be arranged on one inflexible plan, any more than the readers or curriculums of the school can be alike. The country school garden may be expected especially to awaken in the children their first taste for horticulture and for the beautiful in nature, and give an opportunity to individuals to gain a knowledge of fruit-culture, vegetable and flower raising, according as sex, skill and inclination attract to the one or the other. It is not desirable, therefore, that all should learn every thing, which perhaps would not be practicable, and might interfere with the special lessons of the school. And the agricultural "experiment garden," within the school garden, will be of advantage in its whole significance only to those boys who will enjoy the progressive course of agricultural instruction after, they have done with the public school. This kind of instruction is already partly obligatory, and it will soon be so where it is not so now.

The city school garden contains different material of culture from the country school garden. Here especially, roomy, airy, shaded play and gymnastic grounds will compensate the city children for the want of home gardens, and preserve the young from dangerous sedentary pleasures, as well as from the perilous amusements of the streets. Then it will teach them to know the principal trees, shrubs, field, commercial and otherwise characteristic plants of the home region in the spirit of Lüben, without systematic science. This is the least that can be required of either country or city school gardens ; but if each of them offers this minimum, the task of the school garden is essentially fulfilled, and so much is attainable to-day in the city school garden. A somewhat later time will perhaps make the school garden the school of work everywhere, as soon as the teachers are capable of doing it.

As to the rest, it is not to be overlooked that practically the selection of the elements necessary to the school garden is, first, a place for it, and secondly, the means of the given community.

NATURE BETTER THAN PICTURES.

It must not be supposed that a park in the near neighborhood of a city, or a public garden, can render a school garden unnecessary or take the place of it. Such places may suffice for the teachers ; but only personally for purposes of their own culture, not for that of their pupils. Whoever will learn to swim must go into the water, and whoever wishes to know nature must go into nature. If the school wish to teach of natural bodies it must exhibit them, produce them on the spot, and produce them often, and if they are changeable bodies, like plants, they must be observed in their various developments. Nature is better than all the picture books ! It is pitiful to think that many cultivated people in cities do not know even our most common forest trees, whose number does not reach *thirty;* that many city people do not even know how to distinguish the different kinds of grain in the fields ; do not even know that the leaf and flower buds upon trees and bushes are already formed in the autumn, and wrapped in the safe integuments with which nature invests them for preservation against the winter cold.

Excursions for the purpose of learning natural history are very desirable for the city schools, but these are very impracticable in large cities, and would not be sufficient alone to teach any thing more than the most superficial acquaintance with it.

A school garden in the city fills the hearts of the children, even of those who can only see it out of the windows, with transport, and makes them frequent it so much the more willingly. One need but see what joy they have in only a few trees in front of the

school-house or standing in the yard, or when the walls
of the yard or the gymnastic ground are ornamented
with perennial green, or with shrubs in the corners,
or when large flower pots filled with blooming plants
stand around on pyramidal flower stands. So in Vienna
the city pedagogium is ornamented with a little terrace
on the roof, containing a little iron house with a stove in
it for the winter. A still smaller space in some broad
passage-way or in another light room in the school-
house may be appropriated to this priceless purpose.
How much better, when a real, rational, suitable school-
garden is arranged for the city child ! Every tree in the
city is a quiet watch over its health, a source of oxygen,
an ornament, a refreshment. The time will at last
come, when, as in Italy, every city will have its Committee of Improvement, whose task it shall be, after
the example of many cities of North America, England
and France, to beautify the squares and streets with
rows and groups of trees wherever it does not interrupt
traffic. Whoever has once learnt in the school garden
to love trees, will ever after feel it to be an imperative
want to plant and to beautify.

WHAT ONE CITY CAN DO.

Already an area of seventy square metres is offered for
a city school garden in Vienna. Since there will be no
room for woody growths here, they have been raised in
flower pots (according to Prof. Eichert's plan), by a
private citizen or a society (the Horticultural Society),
in time to be loaned to the school. Our park and forest
trees found room on a table at the Exposition, and the
children had an opportunity to learn to know quite dis-

tinctly the bark, flower, leaf and tiny buds. In even
so small a garden the flowers blooming in each month
could be collected in groups. Of course the spring
flowers of the home region and the characteristic plants
of the plain must find careful nurture, even in the very
smallest school garden. A happy collection of the most
characteristic home plants can form a little jewel box
of a garden. So in an alpine region, the most charming alpine plants placed together in an artistic rock-
work in natural groups, make a true feast for the eye of
old and young. A tasteful collection of living mosses
for autumn is a never to be forgotten delight to behold.
When the garden attains the size of 200 square metres,
the woody growths may be collected together in family
pictures. If there is more room still, the plan accompanying this pamphlet can be used essentially for the
laying out of a city school garden. This plan has already been used for a most interesting garden that has
been arranged by Mr. C. Kunze, in Chemnitz, Saxony.
It is 11,000 metres in size ; the ground stock cost
19,000 thalers ; the whole garden 36,000. This creation is for the gymnasium and object school, but it
serves at the same time as a botanical garden for the
public. The gentleman who planned this garden is
such a lover of his kind, that he contemplates making
still another.

A GARDEN IN SAXONY.

In this garden are to be seen statues, a large rockery
for the alpine plants, a pond which furnishes the pupils
with marsh and water plants, a building which serves as
a lecture hall, from whose platform the whole garden

can be seen, a sensible as well as ornamental dwelling-house for the gardener, a sumptuous iron veranda for climbing plants, etc., etc. I do not of course desire so costly and magnificent a garden for a city school. It is not to be expected that it will be imitated in all Europe. It would have too much material for a public school, and would be superfluous as a public school garden.

The question involuntarily arises: Is the school garden practicable in any very large city like Vienna or Berlin?

School gardens are specially desirable precisely here where the children find it most difficult, or indeed not possible, to wander about in the open air with companions of their own age.

OTHER SCHOOL GARDENS.

As long ago as before the World Exposition in Vienna, an interesting experiment was made to create something equivalent to a school garden. The Director Godai of the industrial school in the city pedagogium, arranged the most important home plants in flower-pots and boxes.

But since the exposition, already two proper school gardens have been established in Vienna, one of which was made by altering another garden; the other was created anew.

That hitherto neglected square was altered which is situated in the neighborhood of the Deaf-Mute Institution. In the garden which now occupies this waste place is now a large gymnastic ground, a well arranged garden containing the most important garden and field plants, a tree and vine nursery, a collection of the most important home shrubs, poisonous plants, etc. The class of children for whom this garden is destined need a peculiar care of the sentiments, and it is generally acknowledged the care of plants helps their development very much.

A very useful garden is that of Principal Katschinka, in the 5th district of Margarethen—laid out at his own expense. The present garden was in 1874 on a grass plat. Upon the sod had stood from an early time one great tree and one sumptuous elderberry bush. All the rest was created by Mr. Katschinka. The area of the garden is a modest one—only about 560 square metres—and it contains about 300 kinds of plants, which is a proof that the ground is well used. The most important domestic plants, flowers and forest growths are well represented, so that the children receive instruction from rich material for observation.

The establishment of school gardens in Vienna is possible in many places, for several squares can be obtained for modest little gardens. There are few schools in Vienna that cannot have gardens of at least from five to six square metres in extent. Wonderful as it may sound, it must be said that in this very small space there can be a very pretty little garden.

I have been met with the objection that, even where space for a garden could be found in Vienna, it would be impracticable to have one on account of the multitude of earwigs and wood lice. This difficulty is not of importance. Hard coal ashes used as manure will abolish these pests.

The Common Council of Vienna has referred the question of the establishment of school gardens in the

public and bürger schools of the city to a special committee, by which all necessary measures will be taken,
and all preliminary questions settled before the 28th of
August, 1875, in order to lay out the first school gardens
for the various kinds of school-houses.   This is a fine,
happy beginning.

WHAT TO DO IN SMALL TOWNS.

In the smaller cities, where there is no space in the
direct neighborhood of the school-houses, places must
be obtained by cession or purchase.

The way will be well opened for future school gardens
when in all the recitation-rooms pots of leaf plants and
flowers will be found, which do well in moist rooms inhabited by many people, and when all the windows of
the school-houses, so far as they do not too much im-
pede the sunshine, are adorned with flowering plants.
Cords, or, still better, fine wires must be used to fasten
up the flower pots safely.   Children will be glad to
bring plants from home, to exchange them again for
others when they are out of bloom, and carry home in
the autumn what must be kept there through the
winter.

It is not difficult to take the idea, if one is once convinced of the necessity of school gardens, that a school
garden for girls must be arranged differently in some
respects from one made for boys.   Forest trees can
be grown in both if there is room for them ; but flowers
and vegetables should play a chief part in the girls'
gardens, and the culture of chamber plants should not
be neglected.   Both boys and girls should learn what
belongs in a pleasant home garden ; the boys should

learn to know the wild shrubs and all the important technical and commercial plants, and how to plant and improve trees and take care of trellis fruit.

Let every one answer for himself the question : Will not the habitual frequenting of the city children in the school gardens, and where it is practicable, their occupation in them, in light garden work, tend to create a physically powerful race of men ?

CHAPTER III.

Many friends of schools will perhaps consider it very
difficult, indeed quite impossible, to carry into effect the
ideas thus far developed for the realization of a beautiful and theoretically incontestable ideal, and will look
upon it as a mere pious wish. And this for two reasons. First, because they think the teachers are not to
be found who possess the exalted gifts of the teaching
required for it, and also because the communities would
not be likely to have the means, or the insight, or at
least the spirit of self-sacrifice to carry out and support
such school gardens.

Neither of these things is to be feared. In regard
to the teachers, it is not asked of them that they shall
be learned men, or at least so exceedingly learned as to
be able to know and determine every plant, every animal, or every mineral at sight. There are no such
teachers, and they are not necessary. Indeed they
would not be desirable, since they would have no pleasure in teaching any thing but natural history. But the
requisition that every teacher should know something

(52)

of nature, that every country school teacher should be something of a naturalist, is not a new one ; it has long been expressed by naturalists and pedagogues ; it was the well known judgment of Diesterweg. But as the State has in its hands the teachers' seminaries, it is its business to see that the teachers shall be accomplished in this direction. It emphatically belongs to every teachers' seminary to have a carefully planned, richly endowed school garden. Austria has already set the example showing that such a garden can be established at the cost of a few thousand florins.

The idea of the school garden has now dawned upon the modern state, as is visible in its legislation. The Austrian public school law of May 14th, 1869, by which her legislation has set up a monument for itself of immortal thought, but one not yet sufficiently estimated, says in Section 63 only this : " In every school a gymnastic ground, a garden for the teacher according to the circumstances of the community, and a place for the purposes of agricultural experiment are to be created." Still more significantly and specially were given in the law the instructions for school inspectors of each circle : " To see to it that in the country schools, school gardens shall be provided, for corresponding agricultural instruction in all that relates to the soil, and that the teacher shall make himself skilful in such instruction." Besides this, the school law requires of the teacher the ability to give instruction in agriculture, and the Austrian ordinance upon schools declares expressly in Section 56 : " Instruction in natural history is indispensable to suitably established school gardens. The teachers then must be in a condition to conduct them."

GOOD TEACHERS NECESSARY.

It must not be denied that a great portion of the teachers of the present day are not fitted to conduct school gardens ably. As little can it be denied, that in individual cases, communities or private individuals have bestowed grounds for school gardens which have been afterwards turned into cabbage and potato fields for their own use. Even the laying out of the school garden cannot be left to the teacher, for it belongs to an expert to do that, who may have to act decidedly against a selfish teacher. On the other hand, the private garden of the teacher, which perhaps constitutes part of his lawful income, must not be taken from him to make a school garden. At least, in such a case full compensation must be made to him. In short, there are teachers, where it would least be expected, who would have the selfishness to appropriate to themselves the proceeds of the more modern methods of instruction in natural science, and who yet are too lazy and too great lovers of their ease to look even *once* into a neighboring school garden. But there are enthusiastic and thoughtful teachers who stand in contrast to these mercenaries, and who honor the name of teacher of the public.

It would be very unjust to accuse the communities, particularly the German ones, of a want of understanding of the importance of a school garden ; yet we find ourselves obliged to influence the people by suitable essays and good circulars, and by the spreading of model plans. An interesting example of the interest of many country communities is shown by the market-town of Hainfeld in Lower Austria, which worked out the programme for the school garden laid out there in a manner worthy of imitation. Even Slavic peasants can be warmed up if the right man undertakes to do it. The circle of Mielec in West Galicia, fourteen square miles in extent (a German mile is three English miles, so this would be forty-two of our square miles), is thinking of laying out school gardens for each of its thirty-five schools; and the village of Zlotniki and Chrzastow, besides the little‑city of Mielec, have already established very extensive ones of a landscápe character.

THE QUESTION OF EXPENSE.

The expense of these schemes is by no means so large as one at a distance imagines, as soon as a suitable, not too small territory, is to be had. The work upon the land is often done by the citizens who offer their services for handling and digging without price; and the more readily, because the first work is best done late in the autumn when the farmers have free time to give to it. Larger outlays grow in time by the purchase of fruit trees, which, it is well known, soon give compound interest. Almost all the trees, shrubs, flowers and seeds are acquired without expense from the gifts and exchanges of school gardens themselves. Large landed proprietors, gardeners, foresters, lovers of nature, and public spirited societies are ready and pleased to forward such a public work by their gifts. The royal imperial district chief, Eugen Beueszek, in Mielec, understands all about stirring up enthusiasm for schools. The communities there are erecting numerous new school houses, precisely according to the Austrian model school in the Exposition; large landed proprietors are giving large domains for school gardens, and the wood for fencing them in, in very tasteful patterns, besides plants, small trees, etc. The peasants carry away the bad soil of a school garden, and bring the good earth and work industriously in the laying out. I am in possession of a whole list of demands for school gardens in this district; from noblemen, advocates, clergymen, teachers, etc. I was occupied for several years in the work of the City park at Olmutz, and not only from compatriots, but from strangers at a great distance, who were unknown to me personally, and who did not know the plans, did I receive the most varied assistance. One need only hammer away at such things to succeed at last.

Engineers, architects, gardeners of large gardens, and other cultivated men, willingly draw up a plan if they are asked, and have become interested in the cause. According to my experience thus far, many an able man in every community which expresses the wish is ready to sketch out a garden plan, as soon as one lays before him an outline of the territory with a few strokes, and gives him a description of the place and its surroundings. The space to be taken for the garden offers no special difficulties. Every reader of this essay must see for himself that in most cases the school garden, like the coat in the hands of the tailor, must be cut according to the cloth.

The community must, of course, bear the expense both of laying out and supporting the school gardens; but they will soon bring money to the region, and the teacher whose home garden is quite separated from the school proper, and who has the greatest trouble about it, soon receives half of the net income. The amount flowing into the parish box serves for its maintenance and improvement, and for providing materials of teaching, and other school purposes.

REQUISITES FOR A GARDEN.

The question now arises, What are all the requisites of a good school garden ?

One demand is, deeply dug, well arranged and sanded paths, which shall always be kept clear and in good condition by the children of the upper classes. A school garden which would comprise every thing desirable (that is, such a garden as should be appended to an institution for the training of teachers) should contain

1. A selection of the characteristic plants of the plain and meadow, mountain and wood of the given country.

2. All home evergreen and foliage trees ; at least one sample of each, and all the more important wood-shrubs.

3. A seed nursery for fruit, a nursery for the improvement of wild stock and quinces, a collection of berry fruit and a nursery for them, plantations of precious fruit trees, and especially of dwarf fruit trees, and where possible a trellis for wall fruit and grape vines.

4. An agricultural "experiment garden" of several square metres—that is, an agricultural botanic garden proportioned to the circumstances of the place. A small but very complete "experiment garden" was represented in the school garden at the Austrian Exposition, and gave much pleasure. In the school garden of a teachers' seminary there should be small beds also for the experimental work of individual pupils.

5. In the borders around the "experiment garden" there should be a collection of economical and technical plants of the home region ; stalk fruit, hoe fruit, leguminous plants, and fodder plants, as far as they do not belong in the "experiment garden ; " also aromatic, medicinal, and commercial plants of all kinds.

6. A collection of the chief poisonous plants of the home region.

7. A little kitchen garden with hot-bed or leaf-bed and beds for planting out. The leaf-beds are made in boxes and covered with glass, and are good both for raising seeds and planting slips. They can be used in a window or over an oven or stove, and are made of red clay, which absorbs warmth from the sun even if the glass cover is shaded.

8. In small beds, or singly, flowers, high-bush roses, ornamental shrubs and perennials.

9. A beehive in a distant part of the garden.

10. A small plantation of mulberry trees and bushes (in southern regions) ; and, where it is practicable, a large water basin A fountain belongs to every school.

Since the school has patriotic aims—that is, to build up an army ready for defence and capable of enthusiasm, there should be a gymnastic ground in the neighborhood of the school-house. If this can be within the school garden, it has, like the covered gymnastic hall, found its most beautiful and appropriate location.

EXPENSE AND FEASIBILITY.

A school garden which contains all these requisites does not need an extravagant outlay in order to contain about three hundred kinds of plants for the purpose of instruction and education.

A school garden worthy of the name is practicable on mountain or in valley, on high or low ground, on good or bad soil, near water or remote from water, protected by a neighboring wood or where neither wood, meadow nor tree is at hand. But it must adapt itself to any kind of territory, and be of regular or irregular shape, according to circumstances. To be practicable, it must, above all things, *conform to circumstances*, as well in reference to its shape—which last if not picturesque can easily be masked with shrubbery—as to the practical aims it pursues in reference to naturalizing new, and perfecting already existing branches of industry.

But no one must think that one school garden, in order to work practically, must contain all the advantages that have been enumerated. Such gardens would only be exceptions ; they would be expensive, since they would require the outlay of much money and the services of a specific gardener. In short, they would not be necessary, since the various conditions can and must be essentially distributed in the city and country school gardens.

The given circumstances and the counsel of competent persons must first determine which of these requisitions are pressingly necessary in a given place, which are *very* desirable, which are *most* desirable ; not only what is not immediately necessary but what is impracticable ; in fact, whatever element has been overlooked in this sketch. Above all things, let the largest possible area be given to the school garden, so that its already imagined future improvement may at a later time meet with no difficulties.

DIFFERENT KINDS OF GARDENS.

The different kinds of school gardens may be desig-
ated as : 1. The country school garden. 2. The school
garden for small cities. 3. The school garden for large
cities. The country school garden, and the large city
school garden, may be taken as the two poles.

FURTHER PARTICULARS.

In the country school garden, the central point is
constituted by the "experiment garden for boys," and
the kitchen garden and nursery, which divide the territory into two nearly equal parts. The borders which
encompass the beds can be planted alternately with
dwarf fruit trees, between which—in the kitchen garden—
strawberries and medicinal plants ; and in the "experiment garden," economical and commercial plants will
find their place. Where the woods are very near, forest
trees and bushes need not take up the room in the
garden.

The *large* country school garden requires the beauty
of landscape gardening. In Galizia, through the influence of the author, school gardens have a park-like
character, and only the garden land proper is limited
by straight lines. But in small school gardens, the
ground must be used as far as possible for agricultural
purposes. The paths in small school gardens will
therefore be narrow and straight. The more valuable
fruit trees cannot be in great numbers ; and wall fruit
and grape vines must be left out, as these do not belong
to the first and essential instruction of the garden. If
the garden is small, the beehive must be dispensed
with ; but in the background of all school gardens a

place must be reserved for compost and other materials, and a forcing-bed should be found in the kitchen garden.

In the school garden of the large city, the "experi-ment garden" must be dispensed with. The kitchen garden will only be given to the girls, perhaps, and the nursery must be contained in the very smallest limits, or left out altogether. But all important types of the home flora should be there ; forest trees and shrubs, economical, commercial, medicinal plants, annuals, per-ennials, spring flowers, and plants of the plain. No one will wish for a beehive here. But the gymnastic and playground must be in or near the garden. The garden work and movement in the fresh air are, in a sanitary point of view, inestimable to city children.

CHAPTER IV.

The first point of view, in which the rural population should recommend the acceptance of the school garden, is the elevation it will effect in the condition of the people. How a hundred useful incentives can be given in it, to the future husbandman, has been repeatedly pointed out in this little work.

If the State, the committees, the useful unions, or patriotic men, wish to naturalize and nationalize a new calling which is connected with husbandry, with residence in the country, and chiefly with mother nature, then will the teachers, the men, the school, be exclusively, or, at least specially, in favor of the school garden and a place for it. In the school garden, and by means of it, an abundance of new and practical thoughts will be diffused among the people ; for, in the capability of perfection of the school garden (no moment being left out of sight), lie the seeds of new discoveries and inventions which are to be made by teachers, by compatriots, by the friends of schools and of nature. He who has been happy for eight years of

his childhood in a rational school garden will be thank-
ful all his life for this paradise of his first years ; and
will be earnest to contribute his own mite to the con-
stant perfecting of an institution that has become so
dear to him.   How much will this further the elevation
and nursing of the schools !   Wherever a good idea has
been born or carried into practice in the school garden,
it will become immediately common property ; for the
knowledge of it will spread quickly.   A good garden
will soon have a good reputation, and will be visited by
the neighboring parishes.   The ambition of the outlying
ones will have a praiseworthy zeal and keep watch of it.
The teachers, on their side, will always, in numerous
circles and country conferences, spread the new thought,
and be eager to imitate that which appears no longer as
a mere theory, but as a beautiful idea whose practicability one else might doubt, or esteem too costly ; whose
advantages the individual could otherwise scarcely
measure.   In the school garden an opportunity is offered to place in the hands of the children improved
English and American tools, and to domesticate these
among the whole people to their great advantage.
That the public school garden must essentially further,
directly or indirectly, the husbandry of the country,
needs no farther exemplification.   Where field culture
is changed into garden culture, in the place of one harvest there will be three or four harvests ; the value of
the revenue and the value of real estate will stand in
corresponding relation.

FURTHER ADVANTAGES.

In the first place, a rural population, well instructed
in the school garden, will be capable of carrying on the

occupation of husbandry in a rational manner. A revolution is taking place in the field of husbandry in our day not less striking than in that of national science, industry, and technics ; and has not the school a direct duty to prepare the future husbandsman for his calling?

The time is past in which it could be thought that the husbandman can carry on his work with no other aid than raw experience. Without the knowledge of natural history, or without a general good amount of culture and knowledge, the husbandman is lost, at a period of transition from a method that has been out-lived to one regulated upon firm scientific principles. The husbandman needs to be prepared for his indus-try as carefully as one who wishes to carry on any com-monly called city industry. Should he complain if he lets his little piece of ground lie fallow after, as well as before tilling it ; if he lets his cow go hungry half the winter—chases it from the willow grove in the summer heat, and does not save its dung till after it has become worthless? Not the times nor the accident of another branch of industry is to be complained of, but his own ignorance and want of understanding.

Agricultural unions, popular writings, essays scattered broadcast, model economies, etc., perform only half their task if their theoretic instruction and the exhibi-tion of the object for practical inspection, and the demonstration of the way in which it is to be applied, do not follow directly. And this can be done most ably, most quickly, and most naturally in the school garden, which in certain circumstances—for instance in a poor mountain region, where an agricultural school is impossible in the neighborhood (although just here it would help a most pressing need). The school garden will work even more blessedly than an inferior agricultural school, which in a more favored region the expert of modern times would cast aside.

SOME CONSEQUENCES.

Old ways of husbandry must be changed in many points. In the first place, " the culture of corn must shrink in extent but rise in revenue ; that is, there must in future be more of it, and of better quality, though in a smaller area. For that end it must be cultivated in a cheaper manner, that the net proceeds may be higher and the ground harvest richer." Every husbandman who reckons well will understand this necessity. In the second place, the requisition of the present time on the husbandman proclaims that " in the place of the wheat culture that used to be so imperative, an increased culture of fodder must step in. The breeding of cattle must be improved. The manure must be much more rich and abundant." In the third place, " the demand requires the culture of *commercial* plants wherever it is possible." In the fourth place, modern times demand of the husbandman that he mingle some other occupation with his agricultural one (something that has a . relation to agriculture), in case he fails in his care of his cattle and farm.

A highly important part of the school garden is the cultivation of the agricultural " experiment field " enjoined by the Austrian school law. The pressure of the population upon the means of subsistence in England and Saxony, in the last twenty years, makes it imperative that the same land shall yield at least double the amount it has hitherto yielded. But societies of all kinds, unions, writings, essays, expositions, premiums, schools of industry, itinerant teachers and lecturers, will all come too late if the public school does not give a stimulus to rational improvement in agriculture *to the children*.

Glorious words has Settegast uttered upon this subject : " It cultivates the whole man who must stand in noble self-reliance, that his activity may extend over wide circles those threads of influence with which the welfare of the whole people is interwoven. The clods of the homestead cultivated by him offer a stronghold which is proof against the dark powers of poverty and immorality. In the consciousness of wishing and offering something worthy rests the highest joy of the husbandman. Out of this consciousness he draws the *ideal* contemplation of his calling." Such natures, with such practical, moral and manly views of life, must be formed by the school garden in increasing numbers.

Is a wide-spread proof necessary to show that even the future craftsman, like that city child who frequents no other school than the public school, will gain a hundred incitements directly or indirectly for his future calling from the school garden ? It has been shown plainly that the greatest part of the instruction in natural science has a natural connection with the school garden, but that only through the limiting and concentrating of the material, can that be made fruitful which otherwise it would be better to cast out of the public school as mere rubbish.

BEAUTIFYING THE LAND.

The second point of view which must recommend the general spread of school gardens is the beautifying of the land, which will unquestionably be among their first fruits. Beautiful lands are made still more charming and are more sought when well cultivated ; lands that are not by nature beautiful become more desirable for their own citizens, more attractive to strangers, when beautified by the hand of man. The necessity of planting and improving is excited and increased by the culture of imagination in the child. The sense of beauty, planted in a whole people, is an inestimable capital.

The meritorious idea of founding societies for the beautifying of the land can only be practicable when the children in the schools are won to the beauty of nature. A rural people that has grown up in school gardens will no longer suffer the disfigurement of offal in the streets of a village.*

The Emperor Joseph II.'s idea of planting streets and squares with trees is at last, one hundred years after his death, likely to be realized. How beautiful the villages will be thus ornamented, and what money will flow in good years into the village treasuries ! When the village streets, squares and lanes are enlivened by the beauty of fruit trees, the church-yards will be planted for sanitary and beautifying purposes !

The village streets which are to contain trees must of necessity be broad ; but many walls and fences, many railings and hedges in villages can be covered and ornamented with grape vines and trellis fruit, which will take up little room, and bring in much money.

ITS SOCIAL AND CLIMATIC INFLUENCES.

Austria should be ashamed of the fact that many coun-

* I spare the minute description, and am happy to recognize the fact that no such villages exist in any part of America with which I am acquainted, but they are apparently worse in Austria than in Germany, where no American can fail to be shocked at the spectacles he frequently meets with.—Tr.

tries that lie farther north have roads and lanes planted
with trees, while fertile plains in many regions here,
where valuable fruit could easily be cultivated, are
totally bare.

Soon the beautifying hand of man will work over
home, garden and village. Railroad tracks, as in Bel-
gium, will be rich sources of revenue by the cultivation
of their borders. Many empty bits of land, and bare,
mountain slopes or marshy places planted with bushes
and trees, will lend another physiognomy to the region.
The environs of villages will be planted in many places
with fruit trees, and where this is not advisable, with
forest trees and shrubs'; and many hitherto unprofit-
able and rude landscapes be transmuted into pleasing
and profitable ones. All the by-ways in villages, fields
and turnpikes will be furnished with trees or shrubs.
Living hedges will surround numerous fields, ridges
and dams ; the borders of brooks and the edges of
ponds will be ornamented with the green of fruit trees,
or with forest trees and shrubs. In the cities, trees
will stand before the churches, around the fountains,
upon the sides of the most frequented streets and
squares. There will be promenades where they are not
now thought of. And, where the expense is feared,
people will be astonished at the liberality of the lovers
of man and nature who will furnish the required material, the taste being once excited.

To the most beautiful fruits of school gardens belongs the improvement that will take place in home
gardens. Models of these should be seen in all school
gardens where their is sufficient space. Not only for
their usefulness but for recreation is a home garden
invaluable for a proprietor and his family. When

children are capable of taking part in it, by their training in the school garden, this value will be doubled.
Now they are too often shut out from a participation
with us in its pleasures because the luxury is so expensive
a one that it must be guarded from injury. But when
it is chiefly the children's work, what an added tie it
will be to home !—Tr.] Plans for home gardens should
be given to the children in school, where there is not
space for actual model gardens, and societies for the
beautifying of the land should draw up these plans for
the school gardens. It is chiefly the teachers who issue
from the teachers' seminaries upon whom will devolve
the pleasant duty of modelling, improving and extending
the home garden ; and with them will be found the
treasury of beautiful plans.

EFFECT IN CITIES.

How much more beautiful will life in the cities be,
when the possessors of great dwelling houses can give
their inmates the enjoyment of a home garden, or at
least of a grass-plot ornamented with flowers and shrubs !
And how deeply will it be engraved in the hearts of the
rural population when the peasants' gardens, one of the
most immemorial forms of cultivation, will be again a
common source of enjoyment in places that do not possess it to-day ! In a polyglot kingdom, offering such
manifold stages of material and spiritual culture as the
Austro-Hungarian monarchy, one has an opportunity to
find types of a national home garden stamped by the
whole people. But most home gardens of most nations,
both Slavic and Roman, form a striking contrast to the
ideal attainable under the various given conditions in
modern times. They bear the inherited impress of

hundreds of years, and only the school—that is the
school garden—can bring about a general and thorough-
going change.

A third point of view which should lead school boards
to promote the spread of school gardens, is the necessity of combating our degenerated meteorological and
climatic conditions. The fearful consequences of the
increasing devastation and rooting out of woodlands,
as well as the reckless drying up of ponds and marshes,
increase from year to year in a frightful measure. In
the first place stands the withdrawal of water from
our springs and flowing rivers. Then comes the weeks
and months of alternate, persistent, devastating droughts,
and equally destructive rainfalls.

WHY TREES SHOULD BE PLANTED.

If Schmall's theories of the world-wide fluctuations
of the surface of seas are correct ; and if the scarcity
of water is increasing in the whole northern hemisphere
in consequence of an inexorable law of nature, this
fact must spur us on with double force to combat the
deficiency of water that threatens us with ruin. It is
not to be overlooked, that the impoverishment of Spain,
Sicily, Greece, the Kars (a domain just north of Trieste),
Turkey, Egypt, Mexico, and even of some islands, is
due to this destruction of forests in those countries.

In late years even Austria has brought to mind in a
staggering manner that this evil must be met quickly,
and with comprehensive measures, if ruin is not to en-
sue, and if many a landscape is not to be obliterated
in the course of a few years. For instance, in a part
of middle and eastern Bohemia. The means of redress
are not difficult to find. They consist, apart from the

sparing and nursing of the still standing and new woods, in the vigorous planting of trees on a large scale in the whole land,—indeed in every land. Trees must be planted not only in the streets, where they are for the most part found now, but on lanes, on ridges and hillocks, and on dams. What room the railroad dams occupy! Also, around all springs of water, on the shores of all brooks, on the edges of all ponds, on bare mountain slopes and in all waste places. Street and village lanes and house gardens must be increased in number for this purpose, and should be well planted. This cannot be effected by one effort; and our country population must be gained over to this idea, and be convicted of their indolence.

The preliminary condition of improvement is the systematic foundation of school gardens in the whole land. Even the artificially planted woods, with their ditches to carry off the superfluous water, can never give again to a country that abundance of moisture which, in former times, the original forests distributed far and wide. Still less can large plantations of fruit trees make up for the woods of past times. But, in co-operation with other plantings, they will combat the increasing drought in many countries; and those drying winds which now blow in so many regions over the bare fields and open cultivated plains, to the great injury of the growth of plants, and which carry off from the ground the ammoniacal contents which are necessary to plant life, together with the indispensable moisture, will finally be arrested. With the restoration of the woods, the air and earth will again attain the necessary moisture; the extremes of the differences of temperature between day and night will diminish; luxurious orchards will no longer dry up and be frost-bitten in summer, and the produce of the fields will not prove abortive on fruitful land,—since the woods, as a medium between earth and air, regulate all climatic extremes.

HEALTH CONSIDERATIONS, ETC.

It is not to be overlooked, at the same time, that not only must the land become richer and more beautiful, but also more healthy, when the hand of man produces such extensive sources of oxygen and purifiers of the air.

All the points of view here enumerated—the promotion of the welfare of the people, the beautifying of the land, the combating of our meteorological conditions, etc.—will often in realization be connected with greater objects. This may be shown by an example which will directly illustrate the part that may be played by school gardens in the neighborhood of a great city.

Vienna lies in the midst of a beautiful country on the spurs of the most beautiful mountain chain on the earth. The landscape around Vienna can by no means be called a poor one ; but if you compare the environs of Vienna with those of Paris, an astonishingly great difference may be seen. Paris lies bedded in a garland of gardens ; and the agriculture in the neighborhood of the capital understands how to use all the means of modern science in glorious measure, and to convert the refuse of that world city into a rich blessing of cultivation. Vienna exhibits before its gates many an example of a perverted agriculture, in its fallow land. The cultivation of vegetables in the neighborhood of Vienna is hardly carried on at all. Scarcely any thing but the commonest kinds of fruit trees are cultivated ; pod fruits in very small quantities. The prices of flour and fruit are often shameful ; and so are the prices of other products of the vegetable kingdom. But these high prices for very ordinary goods do not usually profit the producer, but only help the greedy or covetous middlemen. Vienna spends yearly as much as 300,000 florins for the cleaning of the sewers. The fecal matters of the metropolis are wasted in the most grievous manner—for they are conducted into the channel of the Danube. It is a financial misfortune, and certainly no honor, that Vienna was not long ago, like the Italian and French cities, surrounded on all sides by vegetable gardens, fruit gardens and pleasure gardens. The environs of Vienna ought to be so transformed in a wide circuit, in an agricultural point of view, that a whole zone could be cultivated with vegetables, another zone be covered with leguminous plants, and still other zones be divided between the growth and culture of large fruits and grape vines—and of strawberries grown in the open air, which bring so much revenue to many a Thuringian locality. Of flowers and fancy plants, of ornamental shrubs, etc., the same may be said. These zones should be arranged and established by the Royal Imperial Society of Agriculture. All this is practicable as soon as water is brought into the city; but who can believe that this complete revolution can take place in the domain of agriculture, in the environs of Vienna, if the rising generation does not receive the requisite incitements at the school age, and in good school gardens ?

North of Vienna, on the other side of the Danube, stretches the " Marchfeld," an ugly strip of land of a decided *steppe* character, passing here and there through swamps. Its nearness to Vienna, which needs to be provided with the means of subsistence, should spur the inhabitants of this plain to change their territory into a plenitude of gardens. In some parts the ground is good ; in other places the cherries have scorned all endeavors to draw them out of the fruit trees.

The engineer, O. V. Altvatoer, has worked out a plan of a comprehensive State irrigation, and Baron Pirquet has already proved, by an astonishing example, what ' can be accomplished in this unpropitious region by rational irrigation and superposition of manure dissolved in water. Who could deny that all such efforts would be guided and furthered by prudent activity in the school gardens ?

THE MORAL STIMULUS.

The best laws remain inoperative, the best counsels are preached to deaf ears, if, in tender youth, sense and understanding are not enlisted for wholesome innovations. Above all things, we can make youth happy if we give him an opportunity to do garden work. The author knows of a military school whose pupils made a neat little garden, in the great yard, without any special guidance. In all other lands to-day the soldier is still feared by the possessors of large open territory. In France, on the contrary, simple soldiers create charming plantations in tents. There are plenty of barracks in which, without interfering with military purposes, they can be permitted to have little plantations along the walls. The army is called the school of men, and not without justice. Why shall not the soldier, who circulates very much round the world, be the pioneer of so important a thought, which he can put in practice in his distant mountain village? He must be especially the man of deeds. He is called upon like every other citizen to keep sacred the arts of peace. But higher than all else stands the enhanced morality of the people, which can be so well inculcated through the school garden.

CLOSING WORDS OF DR. SCHWAB.

I am conscious of having found, in the idea developed in these pages, nothing that is new. I have perhaps only given expression to what many others feel darkly, to what still others recognize clearly ; and, indeed, what others have partially expressed before me —if not in this connection, or with the same sharpness, a thought which is floating as it were in the air. I have attempted to write as cheap a treatise as possible about my view of the subject, as to what a rational school garden might be able to offer, and what it really will offer. My design is to stimulate to the creation of school gardens fitted to time and place. That the idea here expressed does not possess all the perfection of which it can be imagined capable, is clear to me. I hope, therefore, that other men who are superior to me in endowment, knowledge and experience, may seize upon the idea, improve it and develop it ; but, above all things, may they help to turn the thought into acts!

In Austria, unquestionably, the new school law will be brought into the closest connection with the regeneration of the fatherland. A new spirit will penetrate the public school, and inaugurate a new time.

Already fresh life is infused into the domain of instruction in theory and practice. City and country, every community, the whole world of teachers, every cultivated family, every individual thinking mind, busies itself at present with the first of all the questions of life —the Empire State. Six years have passed since the promulgation of the excellent law, and already a quiet and noiseless, but so much the more persistent process of revolution in public instruction penetrates into the depths of the life of the people. Already we can say that, according to the understanding, the zeal, the self-sacrifice with which every individual as well as every community accompanies this revolution and takes a working interest in it, can the degree of culture, and the morals of the individual and the community be judged.

The erection, preservation and care of the public school is the first consideration of the local authority. It is at present the most important problem of that local authority ; upon its worthy solution depends the whole future of that authority's welfare.

Among all the arrangements of the State, the school takes the front place ; for the school is the nursery of the intelligence, the morality, the industry, the nationality, the justice, the power and the genuine love of the fatherland. That the timely foundation of school gardens, in city and country, will help essentially to further the task of public education, should be clear to every reader of this little pamphlet. Good school gardens will also be sources of health, of spiritual refinement and cheerfulness to the teacher ; they will make it easier to him to teach simply, freshly, lovingly, practically, to educate youth *naturally*, and to make him acquainted with individualities. They will solve the questions in natural history surely and quietly because founded upon the love of work, and therefore upon one of the roots of human activity. The school garden allows itself to be incorporated into every city and country school without disturbing the corporate organism of the instruction. It makes the task of the school not more difficult, but easier; it is possible almost everywhere even if under limitations. That law and prescription cannot enforce a real execution of this material of teaching and education—that almost every thing depends upon the insight and the understanding of the school constituency, is certainly not to be denied. Just as the school-houses of to-day are built differently from those of former times; as school furniture, means of instruction, methods, plans, object of teaching, and whatever else belongs to the school, have changed—so the gardens that here and there have belonged to schools must be changed, if they are to meet the demands of modern times.

OPINIONS SOLICITED.

In conclusion, all teachers and friends of schools, and of mankind, are requested to let the author have the benefit of all their experiences about school gardens. We want their opposing views as well as their propositions for improvement; and their new thoughts, in the interest of the cause, either in the form of letters or through the press. Every critical remark, even to the demolition of the ideas expressed here, will be received gratefully. All the friends of schools are requested to give information to the author of the laying out of new school gardens; and, if possible, to send him a sketch of any such.

And now, teachers, physicians, clergymen, school inspectors, surveyors, parish committees, senators, unions

and societies, friends of youth and of the people, whatever officers or potentates there may be—take unto
yourselves the idea of the school garden, and introduce
it into active life !

The school garden is secured a good future on Austrian ground. The Austrian people, with its warm re-
ceptivity of every thing good, its keen sense of beauty,
and its matchless capacity for self-sacrifice in every,
thing that concerns the schools, will vie with Sweden in
the field of the school garden.

A time will come when it will be difficult to understand how, for centuries hitherto, public school instruction and educational institutions have been able to exist
without school gardens, so simple and obvious is the
idea—but that time will not come of itself.   Hundreds
and hundreds of actively benevolent men must put their
hands to the work for the furthering of this ideal conception—which must be connected with the whole ful-
ness of life, in order powerfully to further the advance
of the people in both the material and spiritual spheres.

CHAPTER V.

Dr. Schwab's little work has been given entire, with the exception of a few paragraphs. Perhaps more that is chiefly of local interest might have been left out, if it had not been for the danger of marring the unity and the earnest flow of the style. As the work of making school gardens is eminently a practical one, I proceed to give suggestions as to what can be done with us at once about them.

It is a singular fact that, while many of our towns have committees for improvement, and the practice of setting out trees is very general in the streets of our country towns, and even suburban cities, the school-yards are bare of every attraction! Nothing gives a stronger impression of the " abomination of desolation " than to enter one of them. But they are generally wide enough to admit of a wide border that can be adorned with the wild-flowers of the neighborhood, which Mr. William Falconer, in the Rural New Yorker of March 30th and April 6th, 1878, assures us grow well when transplanted from the woods to good garden mold. As

few will probably take the trouble to send for these ar-
ticles to the Rural New Yorker, so much of them as
will contribute to the work of the adornment of our
school gardens will be given here.

It may not be known that several hundred plants
bloom in the fields in May, as many others in June, as
many more in July, half as many more in August, and
a few in September. Some of our amateur botanists
have lovingly watched and recorded the birthday—that
is, the flowering day of all these plants. From such a
list we select the prettiest, and those easiest of cultivation for the school garden. Mr. Falconer's love of his
science has gone so far as to induce him to divide them
by their colors, as if he knew school gardens were to be
the next things to be made in this busy world. He has
also preserved the familiar names, which are prettier
for children to know than the botanical ones. The kindergarden, and primary school children at least, can
wait till the days of systematic botany come into their
curriculum, before learning the Latin words that are so
meaningless to them. The chief reason for putting
these wild flowers into the school gardens, is, that they
begin to bloom in April, and run through May and
June, while the annuals cannot be sown in our cold cli-
mate with any certainty of success until June, and many
do not bloom until July. No less than forty wild flowers of all colors bloom in April and May,—bloodroot,
anemones, violets, trilliums, dandelions, buttercups,
marigolds, uvularia, dog-tooth violets, hawthorns, co-
lumbines, ladies' slippers, geranium, Dutchman's
breeches, wake-robin, wild-rose, queen of the prairie,

spirea, wild verbena, Solomon's seal. The children can look for them on their very birthdays, and thus add two months to the pleasures of their gardens.

WHAT CHILDREN LOVE.

It is well to know that many plants, roses, honey-suckles, etc., will go on blooming almost double the time, if the withered flowers are immediately cut off. Children in a school garden will like nothing better than to use the scissors for that purpose. The small experience gained in kindergardens that have a garden (these are very few, alas!) is sufficient to prove how children love the work, and how they carry the love of it away from the kindergarden ; and what *personages* plants become to them, as favorite kittens and dogs do who become part of a family circle. One little fellow whose parents had a magnificent garden, asked the kindergarden teacher, when she visited the family, to go with him to his home garden. He did not take any notice of the splendid flowers that dazzled her eyes as she followed him. At last they came to the spot. The object of interest to the little boy was—a potato vine, on which a few blossoms had appeared. The teacher had advised the children, who had home gardens, to plant each a potato, and watch it. She had no garden in the kindergarden, except in flower-pots in the window, where each had planted a few.peas. These peas were well watched and tended ; and actually bore, not only flowers, but a pod or two, which pods were duly gathered and taken home to be boiled. Another little boy of five, worked an hour or two to dig up and pot a geranium that he feared the frost would spoil in the garden border, and lugged it up to the house with great difficulty. Even

6

in the flower-pots of the kindergarden the turnip can be planted or brought to seed, and the children can be shown, by planting rice or other seeds upon damp cotton in a glass tumbler or other dish, the very process of daily growth ; also that plants can be grown not only from seeds but by slips—and that these must be kept out of the sun, and always moist, until they are rooted. The first new leaf that proves success gives an exquis-' ite pleasure to a child (and not only to a child but to a veteran). The thought, too, that man can help God beautify the earth by preparing the ground properly at a certain place, and keeping all the requisite conditions, may be implanted early in the young soul, which can be shown so many analogies between itself and nature's processes, in the visible world. The very word kinder-garden is a mine of thought.

"What are the flowers of the kindergarden ? These plants that you see are the flowers of the sun," said a kindergarden teacher one day. "The children," was the immediate answer all round. Upon this text what cannot be said ? The whole process of growth in good-ness, with the love of God for its sunshine, can be shown in the daily life of the little kindergarden family ; and those who really know children by observation and study, know that they can take ideas and reproduce them in their own words.

SOME FURTHER HINTS.

The expense of putting a border six feet wide around a school yard ninety-six feet square, is about fifty dol-lars. This involves digging out the sand and putting in the mould. The rest of the adornment can be done by the children of the school. A grass-plot opposite the door to be shaded in time with trees, is a very desirable adjunct to this border as given in the accompanying plan. It will be delightful to the children to have a seat on the grass-plot, where they can eat their lunch at recess, and rest occasionally from their light garden work. An hour a day, including recess, can be given to this work under the superintendence of the teacher ; and soon, doubtless, the children will visit it and work in it out of school hours, especially those who reside near. A day or an afternoon set apart occasionally for visiting the woods in search of plants will soon fill the borders, and annuals can be planted at pleasure. Trees in the corners of the yard and vines over the walls, will make it a charming field of labor for the pupils ; and we will venture to predict that if the teachers make the most of such beginnings, it will not be long before larger domains are provided, and complete school gardens created here as in Austria. No one can read Dr. Schwab's treatise without feeling convinced of the utility of this plan both for instruction and happiness. Some persons have suggested that vandalism will destroy such gardens ; but I think better of human nature. I would not venture yet to cultivate fruits. We must wait for this till school gardens are protected by the authorities, or till the cultivated tastes of the people do the work. But the cultivation of flowers and flowering shrubs will subdue the temptations of appetite, which we know poor human nature cannot resist. Under paternal governments, like that of Austria, it is easy to make sudden changes of this sort ; but where, as in our country, every thing waits for the improvement of public opinion, we must be content to wait for fruit trees in school gardens.

ABOUT.

Every one knows that there is danger of the total rooting out of wild flowers, and ferns, in the vicinity of most of our cities, and even towns. To perpetuate and improve them in gardens is quite a new idea, and worthy of being cherished. Let us try it, and no longer be dependent upon seeds that bid us farewell when they are put into the ground, as most of our purchased seeds do. Those who have hoped for better things from the distribution of seeds from the patent office have been doomed to specially bitter disappointments, as the writer can testify, whose hope is well-nigh immortal, and who has tried them for nearly sixty years ! Even the lawn-seed, that the seed-men assure us to be good, sometimes comes up—chickweed ! A few hardy things come up, perhaps—perhaps not. They more frequently disappoint hope.

A bright farmer is reported in the New York Tribune to test his seeds by fitting and covering a dinner-plate with fine flannel, keeping it wet, and laying his fine seeds upon it. All that are genuine will throw up white shoots ; and he thus judges how much waste he is to allow for in planting. It is well said that the best way to get good seeds is to raise them. Dr. Schwab speaks of seed-nurseries as one of the indispensable things in a school garden that is not too cramped in size. The seed should be gathered from the main stocks of the plants, rather than from laterals. In gardens that are merely ornamental, plants are not allowed to go to seed, because the process of ripening injures the comeliness of the plant ; and, where the plant is perennial, that is to be considered, and many annuals are very unsightly in the ripening season; but a seed-nursery obviates these objections.

ABOUT CATS, ETC.

In soil that is half peat, wild flowers from the woods thrive, if well cared for. Violets and hepaticas, houstonia and meadow pink grow very large, and the violets will give lovely blossoms in October as well as in spring. It seems as if the light of some eyes made flowers grow, but they must be enlightened eyes that see what is to be done, or that find out from the heart that is behind the eyes, and which loves the flowers. Anthracite coal and gas are the arch enemies of house-plants. All sorts of worms must be watched for in the garden, and toads and birds cherished and attracted. Cats must be decidedly abolished. Cats not only drive away birds but scratch up garden borders. It is striking to see how soon birds will return to a garden when several cats have been shot. Kittens are charming as long as their mothers nurse them; but when the latter lose their love for them, and begin to cuff them and turn them upon the cold world for subsistence, look out for the birds! If kittens are begun with early, and judiciously trained, however, they will bring in the birds unharmed, and lay them at your feet, and will gradually learn not to touch them. Such kittens may be allowed to turn into cats. Dogs are dangerous in gardens—particularly if any squirrels linger in the neighborhood, as they do a long time near country residences.

WHITE FLOWERS OF SPRING.

Wood anemona, anemonæ nemorosa, April, May; creeping fleabane, erigeron flagellare, May; sharp lobed liverwort, hepatica acutiloba, May; Solomon's seal, polygonatum giganteum, May, June; bloodroot, sanguinaria canadensis, April, May; rue anemone, thalictrum anemonoides, May; white violet, viola rotundifolia, May; star flower, trientalis Americana, May; large flowered birthroot, trillium giganteum, May; dwarf birthroot; trillium novale, April; snow - drop tree, helesia teltraptria, mountain cinquefoil, potentilla tridentata, June.

WHITE FLOWERS OF SUMMER.

Large white wake-robin, ˏtrillium grandiflorum, June; Pennsylvania anemone, anemona Pennsylvanica, June; spreading dogbane, apocynum androsæ-mefolium, June; dwarf cornel, cornel canadensis, June; lady's slipper, cypripedium candidum, May, June; ragged fringed orchis, habenaria lacera, July; grass of Parnassus, Parnassia caroliniana, July; false Solomon's seal, smilacina bifolia, May, June; white pond lily, nymphœa odorata, June; water arum, calla palustrina, June; arrow head; wax-work, or climbing bittersweet, celastius scandeus, June; spiderwort, tradescantia, virginica, June.

WHITE FLOWERS OF AUTUMN.

White aster, aster trandescantia, July, August; white snakeroot, eupatorium ageratoides, July, August; hairy alum root, heuchera villosa, August, September; hibiscus, hibiscus Californicus, August; hibiscus, hibiscus militaris, August; boltonea, boltonia glastifolia, September, October; white pond lily, nymphæ odorata, June, September; pearly everlasting, antennaria margaritacea, August ; sweet pepperbush, clethra alnifolia, July ; plantain-leaved everlasting, antennaria plantagin-ifolie, August.

BLUE FLOWERS OF SPRING.

Pasque flowers, anemone patens, var, nutalliaria, April ; clover leaf, hepatica triloba, April ; bluets, hous-tonia cœrulea, April ; crested iris, iris cristata, May ; spring iris, iris verna, April ; Jacob's ladder, polemo-nium reptans, May ; violet wood sorrel, oxalis violacea, May ; common blue violet, viola cucullata, April, June ; larkspur-leaved violet, viola delphinifolia, April ; hand-leaf violet, viola palmata ; arrowhead violet, viola sagittata, April ; robin's plantain, erigoron bellidifolium, May.

BLUE FLOWERS OF SUMMER.

Slender blue flag, iris virginica, June ; large blue flag, iris versicolar, May, June ; perennial flax, linum virginianum, June, August ; many-leaved lupine, lupi-nus perennis, June ; prairie clover, petalostemon viola-ceus, July ; western spiderwort, tradescantia pilosa, June, September ; common spiderwort, tradescantia vir-ginica, May, August ; succory or chicory, cichora inty-bus, July, October ; blue-eyed grass, sibyrinchium bermu-diana, June, August.

BLUE FLOWERS OF AUTUMN.

Tall larkspur, delphinium exaltatum, July ; robin's plantain, erigoron belledifolium, fringed gentian, gen-tiana crinita, September ; monkshood, aconitum uncin-atum, June, August ; harebell, campanula rotundifolia, July ; blue asters, aster azurens, curtisii, shortii, July ;

mist flower, concaclinium cœruleum, September ; dwarf larkspur, delphinium tricorne, July ; great blue lobelia, lobelia syphilitica, August, September.

YELLOW FLOWERS OF SPRING.

Dandelion, taraxecum dens leonis, April, September ; golden fumitory, corydalis glaucea, May ; celandine poppy, stylophonum diphyllum, May ; celandine, chelidonium, May, August ; common yellow violet, viola canadensis, May ; downy-leaved violet, viola pubescens, May ; round-leaved violet, viola rotundifolia, May ; marsh marigold, caltha palustris, April, May ; five-finger cinquefoil, potentilla canadensis, April, July ; vent, corydalis aurea, April, July ; early crowfoot or buttercup, ranunculus fascicularis, May ; bellwort, uvularea perfoliata and sessilifolia, May ; bulbosis, May, July ; golden club, orontium aquaticum, May ; yellow adder's tongue or dog-tooth violet, erythronium Americanum, May.

YELLOW AND ORANGE FLOWERS OF SUMMER.

Rocky Mountain yellow columbine, aquilegia chrysantha, yellow-fringed orchis, habenaria ciliaria, great flowered St. John's wort, hypericum perforatum, June, September ; Canada lily, lilium Canadense, June, July ; loosestrife, lysimachia lanceolata, June, August ; evening primrose, œnothera biennis, June ; bellwort, uvularia grandiflora, June ; silver weed, potentilla anserina, June, September ; star of Bethlehem, ornithagulum umbellatum, June ; St. John's wort, hypericum perforatum, June.

5

YELLOW FLOWERS FOR AUTUMN.

Giant sunflower, helicanthus giganteus, May; corn-flower, rudbeckia hirta, June, August; golden rod, solid-ago, many species, August, October; five-finger, poten-tilla canadensis, April, July; wild senna, cassia mari-landica, July; golden fumitory, corydalis aurea, April, July; monkey flower, mimulus ringens, July, Septem-ber; common yellow violet, viola canadensis, May, August; dwarf dandelion, leontodon autumnale, July, August; butterfly weed, asclepias tuberosa, July, Sep-tember; tickweed, coreopsis rosea, July.

RED AND PURPLE FLOWERS OF SPRING.

Rhodora canadensis, May; pale laurel, kalmia glauca, May, June; arethusa bulbosa, May; sheep's laurel, kalmia angustifolia, May, June; pink laurel, kalmia latifolia, May, June; Canadian columbine, aquilegia canadensis, May; spring beauty, claytonia virginica; purple lady's slipper, cypripedium acaule, May; shoot-ing star, dodecatheon meadia, May, June; Dutch-man's breeches, dicentra eximia, May, August; spot-ted cranesbill, geranium maculatum, May; water or purple avens, geum nivale, May; ground or moss pink, phlox subulata, April, May; anemone cylin-drica, phlox reptans, May, June; three-leaved night shade, triiium erectum, May; wake-robin, trillium cer-nuum, May, June; painted trillium, trillium erythrocar-pum, May, June; early wild rose, rosa blanda, May, June; hawthorne, cratœgus oxyacanthus, May; scarlet-fruited thorn, cratœgus coccinea, May; purple violets, viola cucullata, palmata, sagettata, pedata, bicolor, can-ina, stricta, canadensis, May, August; black thorn, cra-tœgus tomentosa, May, June; pink, silene Pennsylvanica, May ; Maryland pinkroot, spigelia Marilandica, June ; May flower, epigea repens, May ; queen of the prairie, spiroea lobata, June ; fringed orchis, habenaria fimbriata, June ; Alpine azalea, loiselauria procumbens, June ; orange-red lily, lilium Philadelphicum, June ; Turk's cap lily, lilium superbum ; wild bergamot,monarda fistula, July, September ; Oswego tea, monarda didyma, July, August ; meadow beauty, rhexia virginica ; loose-strife, lythrum hyssopifolia ; spiked loosestrife, lythrum salicaria ; climbing or prairie rose, rosa setigera, June, July ; swamp rose, rosa carolina, June, September ; dwarf wild rose, rosa lucida, May, July ; sweet brier rose, rosa rubiginosa, June, August ; small sweet brier rose, rosa micrantha ; andromeda, andromeda ligustruna, June, July ; catchfly, silene inflata, June ; catchfly si-lene Pennsylvanica, June ; sleepy catchfly, silene antir-rhena, June, September ; azalea nudiflora, April, May ; azalea viscosa, June, July ; rosebay, rhododendron max-imum, July ; wintergreen, pyrola elliptica, June ; pyrola chlorantha, June, July ; one-flowered pyrola, moneses uniflora, June.

RED AND PURPLE FLOWERS OF AUTUMN.

New England aster, aster Novæ Angleæ ; violet-blue aster, aster spectabulis, September, November ; green aster, aster lœvigatus ; hairy-leaved aster, cordifoleus ; pale-purple aster, miser ; clear-blue aster, amethystimus ; annual aster, linifolinis ; swamp rose mallow, hibiscus moschentos ; blazing star, liatris punctata ; cardinal flower, lobelia cardinalis ; hardhack, spirœa tomentosa, July ; spirœa salicifolia, July ; blue vervain, verbena hastata, July, September ; verbena aubletia, July ; ver-bena virginiana, June, August.

RED AND PURPLE FLOWERS OF SUMMER.

Red columbine, aquilegia truncata, ram's-head lady's slipper, cypripedium arietinum.

CLIMBING PLANTS.

Wistaria, May; trumpet creeper, tecoma radicans, July; wild balsam apple, echinocystis lobata, July, October; common greenbriar, smilax rotundifolia, June, July; Virgin's bower, dematis virginiana, July, August; bignonia capreolata, April; man-of-the-earth creeper, ipomea pandurata, June, August; trumpet honeysuckle, lonicera sempervirens, May, October; yellow honeysuckle, lonicera parviflora, May, June; climbing waxworl or bittersweet, celastrus scandens, June.

FERNS.

In a moist, shady, nook in gardens with peaty soil, Maiden's hair, adiantium, pedatum, July; asplenium ebeneum, asplenium trichomanes, July; asplenium ruta muraria, July; asplenium thelypteroides, July; lady fern, asplenium felix fœmina, July; aspidium achrosticoides, July; aspidium marginale, July; aspidium fragrans; aspidium cristatum, July; aspidium spinulosum, July; aspidium goldianum, July, September; walking fern, camptosurus rhyzophyllus, July; cystopteris bulbifera, cystopteris fragilis, Dicksonia punctilobula, July; climbing fern, lygodium palmatun, July; sensitive fern, onoclea sensibilis, July; cinnamon fern, osmunda cimmonomea, May; osmunda claytoniana, May, fruits as it unfolds; royal fern, osmunda regalis; woodsia ilvansis, June; woodsia obtusa, July; woodwardia virginica, August.

Where there is room for forest trees, the most competent judges, Mr. George B. Emerson, Boston ; Mr. C. F. Sargent, director of Harvard Botanic Garden ; Dr. James C. Brown, of London, England ; Mr. Robert Douglas, of Illinois ; Mr. Budd, of Iowa (see Dr. B. G. Northrop's Economic Tree Planting), recommend the following, either from seed or from saplings.

TREES RECOMMENDED.

Larch trees for durability, strength and resistance to water. This tree is good for railway sleepers, as it holds iron longer than any other wood, and does not corrode it like oak. It attains maturity before the oak. Ten acres of larch will furnish as much ship timber as seventy-five acres of oak, because it can be planted more closely. But the wood loses its hardness in rich Western loam, or in too rich ground anywhere.

The white ash is hardy, a rapid grower, and will bear the bleakest exposures. It must have good soil ; but it gives excellent wood for furniture and farm utensils. The seed is abundant, and ripens about the first of October. If sown in the fall they should be covered with three feet of straw ; if in the spring the seed must be mixed with damp sand. Green bushes will protect the seed in the hottest of summer weather.

MAPLES.

The rock maple grows perfectly in clayey soil. Norway maple or sycamore, stands against Northern blasts and sea-breezes.

Red maple thrives in dry and gravelly soils.

Maples should be planted twenty-five feet apart. Elms should be planted from forty to fifty feet apart. White oak, chestnut, hickory, butternut, white-pine and willows will flourish in New England.

A CATALOGUE OF BOOKS

PUBLISHED AND FOR SALE BY

WOOD & HOLBROOK,

No. 15 LAIGHT ST., N. Y.

Any one of which will be sent by mail, post-paid, on receipt of the price.

"Eating for Strength."

BY

M. L. HOLBROOK, M. D.

INCLUDING

THE SCIENCE OF EATING.

500 *Receipts for Wholesome Cookery.*

100 " " *Delicious Drinks.*

100 *Ever recurring questions answered.*

NOTICES OF THE PRESS.

"The book is for the most part uncommonly apt, coming to the point without the slightest circumlocution."—*New York Tribune.*

"One of the best contributions to recent hygienic literature."—*Boston Daily Advertiser.*

"What is particularly attractive about this book is the absence of all hygienic bigotry."—*Christian Register.*

"One man's mother and another man's wife send me word that these are the most wholesome and practical receipts they ever saw."—*E. R. Branson.*

"I am delighted with it."—*H. B. Baker, M. D., Michigan State Board of Health.*

"The part devoted to innocuous and wholesome beverages deserves warm commendation. Just such information as it contains, widely disseminated, will be a real aid to the temperance cause; better than a thousand overdrawn pictures such as we have *ad nauseam.*"—*Medical and Surgical Reporter, Philadelphia.*

"It would, we believe, be nearly a cure for dyspepsia."—*Druggists' Circular, New York.*

"Its author is so immeasurably in advance of American housekeepers in general, that we hope he may be widely and frequently consulted."—*Christian Union, New York.*

SENT BY MAIL FOR ONE DOLLAR.

Lady Agents Wanted.

WOOD & HOLBROOK, No. 13 & 15 Laight Street, N. Y.

Parturition Without Pain ;

OR,

A Code of Directions for Avoiding most of the Pains and Dangers of Child-Bearing.

EDITED BY M. L. HOLBROOK, M.D.,
Editor of The Herald of Health.

WITH AN ESSAY ON

" THE CARE OF CHILDREN, "

By Mrs. Clemence S. Lozier, M.D.,

Dean of the New-York Medical College for Women.

CONTENTS.

1. Healthfulness of Child-Bearing.
2. Dangers of Preventions.
3. Medical Opinions as to escaping Pain.
4. Preparation for Maternity.
5. Exercise during Pregnancy.
6. The Sitz Bath and Bathing generally.
7. What Food to Eat and what to Avoid.
8. The Mind during Pregnancy.
9. The Ailments of Pregnancy and their Remedies.
10. Female Physicians, Anæsthetics.

To which are added:

1. The Husband's Duty to his Wife. 2. Best Age for Rearing Children. 3. Shall Sickly People become Parents ? 4. Small Families. 5. Importance of Physiological Adaptation of Husband and Wife. 6. Celibacy. 7. Effects of Tobacco on Offspring. 8. Latest Discoveries as to the Determining the Sex of Offspring. 9. Father's *vs.* Mother's Influence on the Child. 10. Shall Pregnant Women Work ? 11. Effects of Intellectual Activity on Number of Offspring. 12. Size of Pelvis, and its Relation to Healthful Parturition, etc., etc.

WHAT IS SAID ABOUT "PARTURITION WITHOUT PAIN."

Godey's Lady's Book says: " We give our cordial approbation to this work, and would like to see it in the hands of every mother in the land. The information it contains is most important, and, we are fully convinced, reliable."

Mary A. Livermore, editor of *The Woman's Journal*, Boston, says: " Your book can not be too highly commended as containing indispensable knowledge for women."

Its gratuitous circulation should be a recognized part of the Woman Movement.—*Index.*

The course recommended can not fail to be beneficial.—*Beecher's Christian Union.*

Glad to see such books from the American press.—*Methodist, (New-York.)*

Contains suggestions of the greatest value.—*Tilton's Golden Age.*

A work whose excellence surpasses our power to commend.—*New-York Mail.*

The price by mail, *$1.00,* puts it within the reach of all.

Address WOOD & HOLBROOK, Publishers,

15 Laight Street, New-York.